Childhood is both a biological phenomenon and a social construct. Research on children is currently of wide-ranging interest. This book breaks new ground in presenting reviews of childhood from four major areas of interest – human evolution, sociology/social anthropology, biological anthropology and developmental psychology – to form a biosocial, cross-cultural understanding of children. The book places a strong emphasis on how childhood, a uniquely human life stage, varies from culture to culture, and on issues relating to the physical and social development of children. It offers examples from developed and developing countries, as well as from other animal species.

It will be of interest to scholars within the fields of human biology, anthropology, sociology, health studies and developmental psychology.

BIOSOCIAL SOCIETY SYMPOSIUM SERIES 10

Biosocial Perspectives on Children

THE BIOSOCIAL SOCIETY SYMPOSIUM SERIES

Series editor: Professor G. A. Harrison, University of Oxford

The aim of the Biosocial Society is to examine topics and issues of biological and social importance and to promote studies of biosocial matters. By examining various contemporary issues and phenomena, which clearly have dimensions in both the social and biological sciences, the Society hopes to foster the integration and inter-relationships of these dimensions.

**Previously published volumes**

1. Famine *edited by G. A. Harrison*
2. Biosocial Aspects of Social Class *edited by C. G. N. Mascie-Taylor*
3. Mating and Marriage *edited by V. Reynolds and J. Kellet*
4. Social & Biological Aspects of Ethnicity *edited by M. Chapman*
5. The Anthropology of Disease *edited by C. G. N. Mascie-Taylor*
6. Human Adaptation *edited by G. A. Harrison*
7. Health Interactions in Less-developed Countries *edited by S. J. Ulijaszek*
8. Health Outcomes: Biological, Social & Economic Perspectives *edited by H. Macbeth*
9. The Anthropology of War *edited by M. Parker*
10. Biosocial Perspectives on Children *edited by C. Panter-Brick*

*Volumes 1–9 are available from Oxford University Press*

# Biosocial Perspectives on Children

Edited by

## CATHERINE PANTER-BRICK

*Department of Anthropology, Durham University*

CAMBRIDGE
UNIVERSITY PRESS

PUBLISHED BY THE PRESS SYNDICATE OF THE UNIVERSITY OF CAMBRIDGE
The Pitt Building, Trumpington Street, Cambridge CB2 1RP, United Kingdom

CAMBRIDGE UNIVERSITY PRESS
The Edinburgh Building, Cambridge CB2 2RU, United Kingdom
40 West 20th Street, New York, NY 10011–4211, USA
10 Stamford Road, Oakleigh, Melbourne 3166, Australia

First published 1998

Printed in the United Kingdom at the University Press, Cambridge

Typeset in $11\frac{1}{2}$/14 pt Baskerville [WV]

*A catalogue record for this book is available from the British Library*

*Library of Congress Cataloguing in Publication data*
Biosocial perspectives on children / edited by Catherine Panter-Brick.
    p.   cm. – (Biosocial Society symposium series; 10)
Includes bibliographical references and index.
ISBN 0 521 57297 5 (hb)
    1. Children.   2. Children – Social conditions – Cross-cultural
studies.   3. Children – Health and hygiene – Cross-cultural studies
    4. Child development – Cross-cultural studies.   5. Human Evolution.
    I. Panter-Brick, Catherine, 1959–   II. Series.
HQ767.9.B54   1998   97–27946CIP
305.23 – dc21

ISBN 0 521 57297 5  hardback
ISBN 0 521 57595 8  paperback

# Contents

6. **The meeting of nature and nurture and the development of children: some conclusions**
MARTIN RICHARDS

# Contributors

PROFESSOR BARRY BOGIN
Department of Behavioral Sciences,
University of Michigan-Dearborn,
Michigan 48128, USA

DR ALLISON JAMES
Department of Sociology and Anthropology,
University of Hull, HU6 7RX, UK

PROFESSOR ROBERT A. LEVINE
Graduate School of Education,
Harvard University, Roy E. Larsen Hall,
Cambridge, MA 02138, USA

DR CATHERINE PANTER-BRICK
Department of Anthropology,
43 Old Elvet, University of Durham, DH1 3HN, UK

PROFESSOR MARTIN RICHARDS
Centre for Family Research, University of Cambridge,
Free School Lane, Cambridge CB2 3RF, UK

1

# *Introduction: biosocial research on children*

CATHERINE PANTER-BRICK

Your children are not your children.
They are the sons and daughters of Life's longing for itself.
They come through you but not from you.
And though they are with you yet they belong not to you.

Kahlil Gibran, *The Prophet*

'Can There be an Anthropology of Children?' This was the provocative title of a paper by Charlotte Hardman, a British social
anthropologist who, in 1973, deplored the 'lack of any recent
anthropological perspective' on children and raised 'the point that
perhaps children could be studied in their own right' (p. 85). A
healthy 'flurry of activity' in the social sciences (James, p. 45, this
volume), coinciding with a rapidly growing literature in the fields
of human biology and developmental psychology, have today established 'childhood' as a topic worthy of serious academic study.

## Child-centred perspectives

There is now a vast literature on children in the biological and
social sciences. Children, however, have often been subjected to a
'top down' approach on the part of adults who shared not with
them the same language or everyday experiences (Fine and Sandstrom, 1988) and whose writings conveyed little of children as
actual people. Cahan et al. (1993), reviewing child studies in history
and developmental psychology, noted 'what we call, for lack of a

1

better phrase, (. . .) the imperialism (. . .) of the adult world on the child's'. They specified: 'There is plenty of adult discourse *about* the child, but the child often is too silent for the historian's usual arsenal of methods' (p. 194).

The same could be said for many studies of children in the fields of anthropology. Within biological and psychological anthropology, there has been an intense focus on children's physical and personality development, but studies have tended to examine the influence of parenting, rather than the child's own behaviours, and relationships with adults, rather than the peers or multi-age groups of friends and relatives. Within the social sciences, also, children and youths have often been 'muted groups', i.e. unperceived, elusive or invisible groups (Hardman, 1973: 85; Morrow, 1995). If not exactly invisible, given the focus of much sociocultural research on childhood (Chapter 5), children have often remained inaudible as their own perspectives and representations of life have easily been overlooked (Caputo, 1995). The exhortations found in the recent anthropological, sociological and child welfare literature – to let children rather than adults drive the focus of research – have given new impetus to current ethnographies of childhood (James and Prout, 1990; Mayall, 1994; PLA Notes, 1996). At the very least, current childhood studies within sociocultural anthropology now make a great deal more room for children's own accounts of their lives and environments – as told by the children themselves (Chapter 3).

## Cross-cultural variability

A very important development in childhood studies has been the documentation of cross-cultural variability in children's experience. Qvortrup (1994: 5) calls to mind recent criticism 'for utilizing the term "childhood" in the singular' – as if there were 'only one childhood. There is, it is said, not one, but many childhoods'. To quote a recent textbook from the social sciences (Jenks, 1996: 121–2), sociological and anthropological research has now 'sharpened a theoretical focus on the plurality of childhoods, a plurality evidenced not only cross-culturally but also within cultures ... the experience of childhood is fragmented and stratified, by class, age, gender and ethnicity, by urban or rural locations and by particularized identities cast for children through disability or ill health'. Similarly, in biological anthropology, a large body of work has focused on how childhood varies within and between societies, to tease the effects of different environmental and biological contributions to children's development (Konner, 1991). Within psychology, cross-cultural research has also 'held a respectable, albeit marginal role' (Woodhead, 1990: 74). In particular, studies of children in the non-Western world have contributed greatly to our understanding of the range of childhood experiences across different ecological contexts (Chapters 3–5). A comparative perspective is also usefully extended to evolutionary considerations of the circumstances which shaped the evolution of childhood in both human and animal species (Chapter 2).

## Biosocial contributions

This volume presents four major perspectives on childhood from four main fields of anthropology, namely evolutionary, sociocultural, biological and psychological anthropology. The authors were asked to provide state-of-the-art reviews of childhood from their own perspectives. Readers will notice that each researcher espouses a particular disciplinary understanding of 'childhood' and, in particular, the consideration of a slightly different age range. While, for example, I adopt UNICEF's definition of children as those from 0 to 15 years of age (pp. 66–7), Barry Bogin considers childhood to begin after the cessation of breast-feeding and to end after 7 years of life (pp. 21–2). Robert LeVine recognises that the terms infancy, young and middle childhood have led to separate academic specialisations within child psychology (p. 103). Allison James, for her part, warns that chronological age may give little indication of sociocultural behaviour, as a 10 year old may well be 'child soldier, factory worker, head of household, school child and dependent offspring' (p. 62). As noted by La Fontaine (1978) and Nieuwenhuys (1994: 24), there exists no obvious cross-cultural age demarcation of childhood, and in many societies the word child designates a kin relationship rather than biological age.

Two authors (Chapters 2 and 3) begin their reviews with the provocative stance that 'childhood has not always existed'. Barry Bogin looks at the current understanding of childhood from an evolutionary perspective, and what can be learnt from a very basic but important question: do other primates and animals have a childhood, or do they merely pass from infancy to juvenile or sub-adult status? In turn, Allison James recalls the argument of Philippe Ariès (1962) who questioned the universality of the concept of childhood, suggesting that in medieval society, children, once weaned, were just 'people', with needs and responsibilities no different from adults. Both chapters reiterate the fundamental point that 'childhood' has varied across time and society.

Their two perspectives, however, while sharing a similar starting point soon diverge to reflect fundamentally different disciplinary interests. Barry Bogin takes an evolutionary viewpoint, considering childhood as a biological phenomenon, shaped by natural selection. He makes explicit the characteristics of human childhood and reasons why they might have evolved (benefits accruing, at least initially, to the parents). He also discusses how childhood, as a stage of development unique to the human species, might have evolved, whether by de novo insertion in the life history of our ancestors, or by modification of the ape-like pattern of growth. His approach is thus a comparative one contrasting human childhood with the period of juvenile dependency in non-human primates. As Lancaster and Lancaster (1983) had argued, the non-human primates, after weaning in infancy, also benefit from a prolonged period of social dependency but 'in contrast to humans the juvenile monkey or ape feeds itself' (p. 36) whereas humans provide for their children at least until puberty. In Konner's words (1991: 427), '*we are the species that takes care of children*' (italics in original).

Allison James takes a very different perspective, concerned as she is with understanding childhood through the lens of children's own actions and conversations, attaching meaning to their many diverse experiences. She argues that childhood is not 'simply and unprob-lematically a description of the early biological development of the human child' (p. 51), but a concept that varies both within and between cultures. Ethnographies from the Inuit, Japan and Zim-babwe, among others, clearly challenge the universal relevance of a cultural model of childhood which has largely been based upon the views of Western adults. Thus in contrast with a Western emphasis on childhood 'innocence', Inuit 3 year olds are deemed able to understand the 'harsh realities of life' (p. 50), and Japanese children are made aware rather than kept in ignorance of potential everyday danger. James goes on to suggest that in non-Western contexts, the social worlds of children and adults may not be mark-edly demarcated, especially as children work along with adults and assume some economic responsibilities. As Postman (1994: xi) wished to argue, 'unlike infancy, childhood is a social artefact, not a biological category'. By this he meant that while infancy is a biological necessity, childhood is a social category with cross-cultural variability.

In the next two chapters, the biological and social perspectives on children are not so demarcated, as indeed the authors advocate a contextual or ecological approach to considerations of a child's physical and psychological development. They here bridge a con-cern with cross-cultural measurements of child development with consideration of the range of specific cultural attitudes relating to childcare and the nature of environmental constraints affecting sur-vival, health, well-being or success evaluated in social or edu-cational terms.

The brief of my own chapter centres on children's health and well-being. I focus on ways in which biological anthropologists studying modern human populations have conducted cross-cultural studies of children, and methodologies most suitable for working with children. To appraise child health, heavy reliance is placed on a number of trusted indicators borrowed from the fields of demography, auxology (growth), nutrition and epidemiology. In reviewing some of the uses made of such indicators, I emphasise the importance of a contextual approach that focuses on children's specific environments, such as the significance of household composition to explain growth retardation. I argue that standard indicators of ill-health, while useful, often focus on measuring final outcomes (death, slow growth, malnutrition) rather than examining the long-term processes by which children cope with different environments (adaptive behaviour, vulnerability or resilience). Thus I draw attention to the importance of documenting children's behaviours and levels of physical activity in a range of physical and social environments. I caution that too narrow a focus on a child's physical health, often espoused in Western biomedical practice, may jar with other, significant community concerns, centred on the perceived contribution of the child to a household's socioeconomic activities. I also review some of the pioneering work done on stress and well-being, a dimension less easy to measure and conceptualise than frank ill-health, but which offers exciting perspectives for future research.

Robert LeVine also gives consideration to the range of cultural and ecological contexts affecting child development. He begins by reviewing the 'distinctive but limited role' of cross-cultural (anthropological) research in the field of child psychology (p. 105), and the debate of views regarding the extent to which nature and nurture are thought to construe child development. In his cross-cultural comparison of infants in Kenya, the USA and Germany, LeVine examines the range of environmental contexts as well as the specific nature of parental goals and caregiving behaviours that influence child development. Thus Gusii children in Kenya are raised to be quiet and obedient, while North American counterparts are 'precociously' self-confident and socially engaged, and German children self-reliant or 'unspoilt' – the result of plain parental neglect from the viewpoint of American parents! Cultural 'priming' is also noted in Japan, where children are taught to avoid confrontation and acquire empathy for others. These observations are integrated in a model of environmental optimisation whereby infant care behaviours are geared to achieve culturally specific priorities for child development (to realise concerns for basic survival for the Gusii, success in pediatric education for North Americans, and independence for the Germans).

This volume arose from a workshop of the Biosocial Society

which aims to promote discussion of issues relevant to both biological and social domains. Childhood is obviously an important topic
for a number of academic fields of study. Yet as candidly stated by
the participants of a previous multi-disciplinary workshop on children (Elder et al., 1993: 175), 'the disciplines have different stories
to tell', and at the workshop itself, 'a certain amount of puzzlement
resulted when (despite being interested in a common subject) we
were rowing hard but in different directions'. Certainly in this
volume, the perspectives presented on children overlap, but are
diverse indeed. It is hoped that these contributions will inform readers of current thinking developed in the biosocial sciences and per-
suade them to wander beyond the confines of their particular interest or discipline.

Indeed, in the final chapter of this volume, the discussant Martin
Richards focuses attention on the need for greater integration
between biological and social fields of study. His analogy is one of
a journey through the landscape of childhood, viewed by passengers on a train seated by different windows. While a particular
aspect of the scenery, or academic discipline, can be charted from
a given window, the total landscape can only be viewed by integrating the different maps drawn from each side of the train (pp. 131–
2). The contribution raises theoretical issues concerning our
approaches to understanding the processes of biological and social
development. It rejects the traditional conceptualisation of nature
and nurture as separate domains of child development, to advocate
instead an epigenetic approach that recognises the interaction of
genetic and environmental influences shaping the development of
individual children.

In brief, this volume aims to provide undergraduate and post-
graduate students with substantive and accessible reviews of current
academic research on childhood. It targets an audience in the
broad field of human sciences, including social anthropology, sociology, human evolution, human biology, human ecology, health
studies and developmental psychology. In light of the emergence of
children's issues as a topic of public (Black, 1995) as well as academic concern, it is particularly important to foster a multi-
disciplinary, cross-cultural understanding of childhood.

## Acknowledgement

Grateful acknowledgement is made to the Parkes Foundation for a grant which facilitated the publication of this book.

## References

Ariès, P. (1962). *Centuries of Childhood*. London: Cape.

Black, M. (1995). *Children First – The Story of UNICEF, Past and Present*. Oxford: Oxford University Press.

Cahan, E., Mechling, J., Sutton-Smith, B. and White, S. H. (1993). The elusive historical child: ways of knowing the child of history and psychology. In: *Children in Time and Place – Developmental and Historical Insights*, ed. G. H. Elder, J. Modell and R. D. Parke, pp. 192–223. Cambridge Studies in Social and Emotional Development. Cambridge: Cambridge University Press.

Caputo, V. (1995). Anthropology's silent 'others': a consideration of some conceptual and methodological issues for the study of youth and children's cultures. In: *Youth Cultures – A Cross-cultural Perspective*, ed. V. Amit-Talai and H. Wulff, pp. 19–42. London: Routledge.

Elder, G. H., Modell, J. and Parke, R. D. (1993). *Children in Time and Place – Developmental and Historical Insights*. Cambridge Studies in Social and Emotional Development. Cambridge: Cambridge University Press.

Fine, G. A. and Sandstrom, K. L. (1988). *Knowing Children: Participant Observation with Minors*. London: Sage Publications.

Hardman, C. (1973). Can there be an anthropology of children? *Journal of the Anthropological Society of Oxford*, **4**, 85–99.

James, A. and Prout, A. (eds). (1990). *Constructing and Deconstructing Childhood: Contemporary Issues in the Sociological Study of Childhood*. London: Falmer Press.

Jenks, C. (1996). *Childhood*. London: Routledge.

Konner, M. (1991). *Childhood*. Boston: Little, Brown and Company.

La Fontaine, J. S. (1978). *Sex and Age as Principles of Social Differentiation*. London: Academic Press.

Lancaster, J. B. and Lancaster, C. S. (1983). Parental investment: the hominid adaptation. In: *How Humans Adapt: A Biocultural Odyssey*, ed. J. Ortner, pp. 33–56. Washington DC: Smithsonian Institution Press.

Mayall, B. (ed.). (1994). *Children's Childhoods: Observed and Experienced*. London: Falmer Press.

Morrow, V. (1995). Invisible children? Toward a reconceptualization of childhood dependency and responsibility. *Sociological Studies of Children*, **7**, 207–30.

Nieuwenhuys, O. (1984). *Children's Lifeworlds – Gender, Welfare and Labour in the Developing World*. London: Routledge.

PLA Notes. (1996). *Special Issue on Children's Participation*. London: International Institute for Environment and Development.

Postman, N. (1994). *The Disappearance of Childhood*. New York: Vintage Books.

Qvortrup, J. (1994). Childhood matters: an introduction. In: *Childhood Matters – Social Theory, Practice and Politics*, ed. J. Qvortrup, M. Bardy, G. Sgritta and H. Wintersberger, pp. 1–24. Aldershot: Avebury.

Woodhead, M. (1990). Psychology and the cultural construction of children's needs. In: *Constructing and Deconstructing Childhood: New Directions in the Sociological Study of Childhood*, ed. A. James and A. Prout, pp. 60–77. London: Falmer Press.

2

# Evolutionary and biological aspects of childhood

BARRY BOGIN

## Introduction

In this chapter, the following arguments are presented: (1) *Homo sapiens* is the only living species that has a childhood stage of biological and social development; (2) Childhood was inserted de novo into hominid life history sometime within the last two million years, perhaps during the time of our *Homo habilis* ancestor; (3) Childhood provides 'extra' time for brain development and learning; however, childhood did not evolve by any process that merely prolonged the pre-existing infant or juvenile stages of primate growth and development (neoteny or hypermorphosis).

In evolutionary thinking, the initial selective value of a childhood stage of development may be closely related to parental strategies to increase reproductive success. Childhood allows a woman to give birth to new offspring and provide care for existing dependent young. Childhood also allows for increased developmental plasticity leading to an improved fit between the human phenotypes and local environments. Understanding the nature of childhood helps to explain why human beings have lengthy development and low fertility. For most species this would equate with low reproductive success. Due in part to the unique childhood stage, however, human parents raise a greater percentage of offspring to adulthood than any other species.

## Intimations of immortality

My heart leaps up when I behold
A rainbow in the sky:
So was it when my life began;
So is it now I am a man;
So be it when I grow old,
Or let me die!
The child is father of the man;
And I could wish my days to be
Bound each to each by natural piety.

William Wordsworth wrote these words of innocence and hope in 1802. Set in the scientific–reductionist language of the late twentieth century some might interpret Wordsworth to mean that only through our offspring can we, as individuals with our so-called 'selfish genes', hope to achieve any sort of physical immortality. Yet, *Homo sapiens* is a most unusual species in this regard. Allison Jolly, author of *The Evolution of Primate Behavior*, states that, '. . . human evolution is a paradox. We have become larger, with long life and immaturity, and few, much loved offspring, and yet we are more, not less adaptable'. In an attempt to resolve the paradox of human evolution and our peculiar life history, Jolly concludes in the next sentence that, '. . . mental agility buffers environmental change and has replaced reproductive agility' (1985: 44). The reference to reproductive agility means that we are a reproductively frugal species compared with those that lavish dozens, hundreds or thousands of offspring on each brood or litter. A paradox remains, however, for the emphasis on 'brain power' rather than reproduction is an apparent exception to Darwin's rules of natural selection. Evolutionary success is traditionally measured in terms of the number of offspring that survive and reproduce. Biological and behavioural traits do not evolve by natural selection unless they confer upon their owners some degree of reproductive advantage in terms of survivors a generation or more later. If we are truly interested in our immortality, or at least that of our DNA, then why do we not produce more offspring, instead of a few mentally agile offspring?

Another question is, why do our offspring take so long to reach

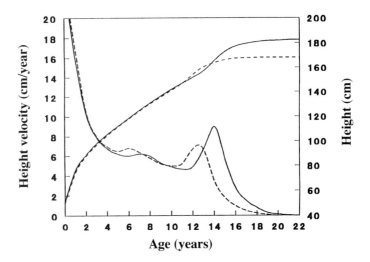

Figure 2.1. Idealised (see text) mean velocity and distance curves of growth in height for healthy girls (dashed lines) and boys (solid lines) showing the postnatal stages of the pattern of human growth. Note the spurts in growth rate at mid-childhood and adolescence. Both spurts occur earlier, on average, for girls than for boys. The childhood and adolescent growth spurts are unique to the human species.

reproductive age? After all, our physical immortality requires that we have grandchildren, great grandchildren, and so on. Yet, we take two decades of postnatal development to reach reproductively successful adulthood. Moreover, our path from birth to maturity is sinuous, meandering through alternating periods of rapid and relatively slow development. This may be seen in the examples of the distance and velocity curves of growth for healthy children illustrated in Figure 2.1. Why do our offspring not take a more direct and rapid path to maturity?

This chapter attempts to answer these questions and paradoxes in terms of the evolution of human growth and development. Throughout the chapter the focus is on children and childhood. It is argued here that childhood is a unique stage of the human life cycle, a stage not to be found in the life cycle of any other living mammal.

# Evolution of human ontogeny

How did the human pattern of growth evolve? To ask this question is nearly the same as asking how the human species evolved. The ontogeny of an individual organism is, metaphorically, a scrapbook of the biological history of that species. Ontogeny refers to the process of growth, development and maturation of the individual organism from conception to death. The metaphor of a scrapbook is used here to indicate that embodied in ontogeny are fragments of our biological past, fragments that have been pasted into our book of life history. These scraps of biological history, which are technically called structural and regulatory genes, are somewhat like scrap metal. Such metal is collected to be reworked in new forms and newer, more useful objects. During hominid evolution the form and function of our ancestors' structural and regulatory DNA was reworked to produce the genetic basis for the ontogeny of the human species.

The literature is replete with proposals for how the reworking occurred. One tradition in the study of human evolution looks for a single major cause. It has been argued that humans evolved when we became big-brained apes, terrestrial apes, killer apes, hunting apes, aquatic apes, tool-making apes, symbolic apes, monogamous apes, food sharing apes and, even, apes with ventral–ventral copulatory behaviour. None of these, or any other single factor hypothesis, proves to be helpful in understanding human evolution, for a non-human primate exception can always be found. Another tradition looks instead at the pattern of ontogeny. In *Size and Cycle*, J. T. Bonner (1965) develops the idea that the stages of the life cycle of an individual organism, a colony or a society are, '. . . the basic unit of natural selection'. Bonner's focus on life cycle stages follows from the research of several nineteenth- and twentieth-century embryologists who proposed that speciation is often achieved by altering rates of growth of existing life stages and by adding or deleting stages.

A history of research on life cycle evolution was published by S. J. Gould in *Ontogeny and Phylogeny* (1977). Gould handily summarises the mechanisms for biological change over time by stating,

'Evolution occurs when ontogeny is altered in one of two ways: when new characters are introduced at any stage of development with varying effects upon subsequent stages, or when characters already present undergo change in developmental timing. Together, these two processes exhaust the formal content of phyletic change . . .'. Gould contends that it is the second process, called heterochrony, that accounts for human evolution. Gould explains that there are several types of heterochronic processes, but only one accounts for human evolution. This is neoteny, defined in the glossary of Gould's book as, 'Paedomorphosis (retention of formally juvenile characters by adult descendants) produced by retardation of somatic development'. In a subsequent publication Gould provides a somewhat more readable definition, 'In neoteny rates of development slow down and juvenile stages of ancestors become adult features of descendants' (Gould, 1981: 333).

In *Heterochrony: The Evolution of Ontogeny*, Michael McKinney and Kenneth McNamara (1991) argue against neoteny and for another type of heterochronic process to account for human growth and evolution, namely hypermorphosis. They state their position as follows, 'Neoteny is the process of growing slower. Yet humans do not grow particularly slow (relative to either chimp or our ancestors . . .). What we do is delay the offset of virtually all dvelopmental events (growth phases) so that each phase is longer. This is hypermorphosis . . .' (p. xi). Hypermorphosis has also been invoked to account for the evolution of human cognitive capacities (Parker, 1996). To quote Parker, 'Cognitively, humans are overdeveloped rather than underdeveloped apes' (p. 377). Elizabeth Vrba (1996) agrees that hypermorphosis is the key process in human evolution. Many of the 'ancestral growth profiles' of the hominids (pre-human ancestors) are, according to Vrba, still to be found in the great apes. She states, 'I do not imply that the chimpanzee itself is ancestral, but only that its growth profile resembles that of the common ancestor' (1996: 17). Vrba predicts that by maintaining chimpanzee growth rates for legs, arms, torso, skull, brain, etc. and prolonging the total time for growth, it is possible to derive a modern human morphology from an African pongid morphology.

## Critiques of heterochrony

Shea (1989) published the most cogent analysis to date that rejects both neoteny or hypermorphosis as a 'grand unification theory' for all of human growth and evolution. In Figure 2.2 are illustrated Shea's estimates for body size and shape as a consequence of neoteny and two types of hypermorphosis. None of these acting as a single process can produce the human adult size and shape from the human infant size and shape. To accomplish this required, in Shea's view, several genetic changes or adjustments during human evolution. These would be the changes of adjustments to the structural and regulatory DNA that are preserved in the 'scrapbook' of human ontogeny. As the hormones that regulate growth and development are, virtually, direct products of DNA activity, Shea proposes that the best place to look for evidence of the evolution of ontogeny is in the action of the endocrine system. According to Shea and others (Bogin, 1988) the endocrine differences between humans and other primates negate neoteny or hypermorphosis as unitary causal processes and instead argue for a multi-process model for human evolution. For example, Bogin (1988) shows that human and chimpanzee males have relatively small differences in testosterone levels during puberty, but relatively large differences in the rate of growth of arms and legs at that time, with humans growing about five times faster than the chimpanzee. The heterochronic models of neoteny and hypermorphosis predict that a greater or lesser amount of time for growth produces the differences in size and shape between humans and chimpanzees. The empirical data gathered from growth and endocrine research, however, show that it is the sensitivity of specific skeletal parts to testosterone, determined by DNA and cellular activity, that results in the differences in limb size and shape between adult humans and chimpanzees. The time available for growth is largely irrelevant.

## The case for de novo childhood

Forgotten by all parties in the litigation surrounding heterochrony is that there is another process by which evolution works. I requote

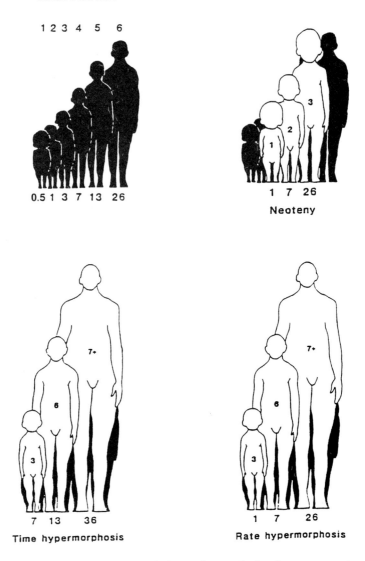

Figure 2.2. Silhouettes of size and shape change during human growth. Numbers under silhouettes indicate age in years. Numbers above or on silhouettes indicate relative shape. Top left: actual size and shape change during normal human development. Top right: neoteny, note that at adult size shape 3 is still maintained. Bottom left: time hypermorphosis, the growth period is extended to 36 years yielding a peramorphic giant (size and shape of the descendant beyond that of the ancestor). Bottom right: rate hypermorphosis, growth ends at age 26 but proceeds at a faster rate producing another peramorphic giant. Note that in both cases the adult shape at 7+ is outside the range of normal development. From Shea (1989) with permission.

Gould as he stated most succinctly that, 'Evolution occurs when ontogeny is altered in one of two ways': the first is, '. . . when new characters are introduced at any stage of development with varying effects upon subsequent stages. . .' Much of human evolution, especially the evolution of childhood, is the result of the introduction of new life stages into the general pattern of primate growth and development.

Let us first look at the general mammalian and primate patterns of growth and then compare these with the human pattern. The majority of mammals progress from infancy to adulthood seamlessly, without any intervening stages, and while their growth rates are in decline (Brody, 1945; Bertalanffy, 1960). This pattern of postnatal growth is illustrated in Figure 2.3 using data for the mouse. Highly social mammals, such as wolves, wild dogs, lions, elephants and the primates, postpone puberty by inserting a period of juvenile growth and behaviour between infancy and adulthood. Juveniles may be defined as, '. . . prepubertal individuals that are no longer dependent on their mothers (parents) for survival' (Pereira and Altmann, 1985: 236). This definition is

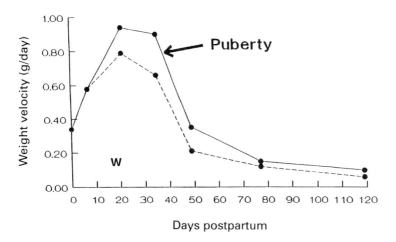

Figure 2.3. Velocity curves for weight growth in the mouse. In both sexes (—●—, males; – –●– –, females) puberty (vaginal opening for females or spermatocytes in testes of males) occurs just after weaning and maximal growth rate. Weaning (W) takes place between days 15 and 20. After Tanner (1962).

derived from ethological research with social mammals, especially non-human primates, and applies to the human species as well. In the highly social mammals, puberty occurs while the rate of growth is still decelerating and there is no readily detectable growth spurt in skeletal dimensions (Figure 2.4, but see Tanner et al., 1990, who find that one sample of captive rhesus monkeys have a skeletal growth spurt at puberty that is larger than the human adolescent spurt).

Human growth and development from birth to reproductive maturity may be characterised by five stages: (1) infancy, (2) child-hood, (3) juvenile, (4) adolescence and (5) adulthood (Bogin, 1988, 1995). Thus, humans add childhood and adolescence to the pattern found for primates and other highly social mammals. Each of the human stages of growth can be defined by clear biological and behavioural characteristics, especially those related to the rate of growth, feeding and reproductive behaviour.

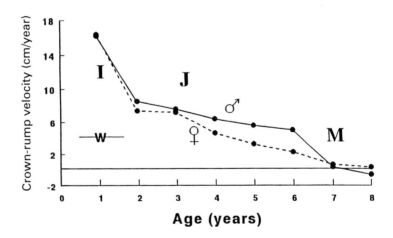

Figure 2.4. Baboon crown–rump length velocity. The letters indicate the stages of growth: I: infancy; J: juvenile; M: sexual maturity. In the wild the weaning (W) process begins as early as 4 months of age and ends by 12–18 months (Altmann, 1980). Puberty begins at about 3.5 years in females (– –●– –) and 4.5 years in males (—●—) and ends by about 6 years in both sexes. Redrawn with some data smoothing from Coelho (1985). The pattern of growth for other primate species, including chimpanzees, are similar to these rates for the baboon (Bogin, 1988: 57–68).

# Rate of growth

Changes in the velocity of growth from birth to adulthood signal the transitions between these five developmental stages. Idealised (the curves are the ideal form of the growth curve for human beings based on the growth of healthy people) velocity curves are presented in Figure 2.1. During infancy growth rate plummets, followed by a period of slower velocity decline in childhood. The end of childhood is often marked by a small increase in velocity, the mid-growth spurt (Tanner, 1947). The mid-growth spurt is associated with an endocrine event called adrenarche, the progressive increase in the secretion of adrenal androgen hormones. Adrenarche is found only in chimpanzees and humans, and the mid-growth spurt is unique to humans. As the childhood stage of growth is also unique to humans, the biology of adrenarche is worthy of investigation. As of this writing, the mechanism controlling the adrenarche is not understood as no known hormone appears to cause it.

Following childhood, growth rate declines further during the juvenile stage. The onset of adolescence is marked by a sudden and rapid increase in growth rate, which peaks at a level unequalled since early infancy. In biological terms, adulthood begins when growth of the skeleton stops.

# Feeding and breeding

Changes in human feeding and reproductive behaviour complement the pattern of human growth velocity. As for all mammals, human infancy is the period when the mother provides all or some nourishment to her offspring via lactation. The infancy stage ends when the young mammal is weaned. Weaning is defined here as the termination of lactation by the mother (other researchers may define weaning as the process of shifting from lactation to eating solid foods). In human societies the age at weaning varies greatly. Industrialised societies provide a poor indication of weaning age because bottle feeding and the manufacture of 'baby foods' allow either early termination of breast-feeding or no breast-feeding at all. Pre-industrialised human societies provide a better indication of biological constraints on the age at weaning, and hence the transition from infancy to childhood. One study finds that the termination of breast-feeding occurs at a median age of 36 months in these societies (Dettwyler, 1995). Another review of such research (Lee et al., 1991) finds that in so-called 'food enhanced' societies, those where nutritional intake is good, weaning takes place as early as 9 months of age. In 'food limited' societies, where chronic undernutrition occurs, weaning takes place at 36 months. There are two fascinating corollaries of this comparison. The first is that in both the 'food enhanced' and the 'food limited' societies the mean weight of weaned infants is about the same, 9.0 kg and 9.2 kg, respectively, or about 2.7 times the birth weight (Lee et al. assume a mean birth weight of 3400 g for full-term human beings). The second is that some solid foods are introduced into the diet when the infant achieves about 2.1 times the birth weight. In this and in a subsequent paper Lee and colleagues (Lee et al., 1991; Bowman and Lee, 1995) compared the human data with data from 88 species of large-bodied mammals (32 non-human primates, 29 ungulates, 27 pinnipeds). They found that for all these species solid food is introduced, again, at about 2.1 times the birth weight, but weaning takes place when the infant achieves between 3.2 and 4.9 times the birth weight. For all primates the mean value is 4.6 times the birth weight (range 2.3 for *Micropithecus talapoin* to 9.4 for *Gorilla gorilla*). The other great apes wean at the following multiples of birth weight: *Pan troglodytes*, 4.9; *P. pariscus*, 6.1; *Pongo pygmaeus*, 6.4.

Thus, humans are similar to other mammals in that we introduce solid foods at about 2.1 times the birth weight. Humans are unlike other mammals, however, even other species of primates, in that pre-industrial and traditional societies, including 'food limited' groups such as !Kung hunter–gatherers, wean at a relatively early stage of growth – before reaching three times the birth weight. The reasons for the 'early' human weaning are related to the large size and rapid rate of growth of the human brain, the reproductive behaviour of human women and the advantages accruing to both parents and young by adding a childhood stage of growth to human ontogeny. These reasons are described in greater detail in later sections of this chapter. Before moving on to this discussion, however, the feeding and reproductive characteristics of the stages of human growth following infancy are described briefly.

Childhood is defined here as the period following weaning, when the youngster still depends on older people for feeding and protection. Children require specially prepared foods due to the immaturity of their dentition and digestive tracts, and the rapid growth of their brain (Figure 2.5). Leonard and Robertson (1992) estimate that, 'A human child under the age of 5 years uses 40–85% of resting metabolism to maintain his/her brain. Therefore, the consequences of even a small caloric debt in a child are enormous given the ratio of energy distribution between brain and body' (p. 191). These constraints of a small digestive system, immature dentition and calorie demanding brain necessitate a diet low in total volume but dense in energy, lipids and proteins. Children are also especially vulnerable to predation because of their small body size and to

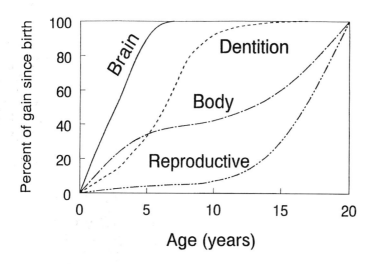

Figure 2.5. Growth curves for different body tissues. The 'Brain' curve is for total weight of the brain (Cabana et al., 1993). The 'Dentition' curve is the median maturity score for girls based on the seven left mandibular teeth (incisors 1 and 2, canine, premolar 1 and 2, molars 1 and 2) using the reference data of Demirjian (1978). The 'Body' curve represents growth in stature or total body weight and the 'Reproductive' curve represents the weight of the gonads and primary reproductive organs (Scammon, 1930).

many diseases, and thus require protection. Given all of this, there is no society in which children survive if deprived of this special care in feeding and protection which must be provided by older individuals.

Important developments that allow children to progress to the juvenile stage of growth and development are the eruption of the first permanent molars and completion of growth of the brain (in weight). The first molar eruption takes place, on average, between the ages of 5.5 and 6.5 years in most human populations (Jaswal, 1983; Smith, 1992). Recent morphological and mathematical investigations show that brain growth in weight is complete at a mean age of 7 years (Cabana et al., 1993). At this stage of development the child becomes much more capable dentally of processing an adult-type diet (Smith, 1991a). Furthermore, nutrient requirements for the maintenance and the growth of both brain and body diminish to less than 50% of total energy needs. Finally, cognitive capacities mature to new levels of self-sufficiency, e.g. shifting from the pre-operational to concrete operational stage using the terminology of Piaget (Piaget and Inhelder, 1969).

As an aside, many sources from Egyptian times to the nineteenth century mention that 'childhood' occupies the first 6 to 7 years of life (Boyd, 1980). To quote Wordsworth again,

> Behold the Child among his newborn blisses,
> A six-years' Darling of a Pygmy size!
> See, where 'mid work of his own hand he lies,
> Fretted by sallies of his mother's kisses,
> With light upon him from his father's eyes!
>
> from Ode: Intimations of Immortality (1802–4)

The child then progresses to the juvenile stage. Ethnographic research shows that juvenile humans have the physical and cognitive abilities to provide much of their own food and to protect themselves from predation and disease (Weisner, 1987; Blurton Jones, 1993). In girls, the juvenile period ends, on average, at about the age of 10 years. This is 2 years before it usually ends in boys, the difference reflecting the earlier onset of puberty in girls.

Human adolescence begins with puberty, marked by some visible sign of sexual maturation such as pubic hair (indeed the term is derived from the Latin *pubescere*: to grow hairy). The adolescent stage also includes the development of the secondary sexual characteristics and the onset of adult patterns of sociosexual and economic behaviour. These physical and behavioural changes at puberty occur in many species of social mammals. What makes human adolescence different is that during this life stage both boys and girls experience a rapid acceleration in the growth of virtually all skeletal tissue – the adolescent growth spurt. The evolution of human adolescence and the growth spurt is treated in detail in other publications (Bogin, 1994a, 1995; Bogin and Smith, 1996).

Adolescence ends and early adulthood begins with the completion of the growth spurt, the attainment of adult stature, the completion of dental maturation (eruption of the third molar, if present) and the achievement of full reproductive maturity (Figure 2.5). The latter includes both physiological, socioeconomic and psychobehavioural attributes which all coincide, on average, by about age 19 years in women and 21–25 years of age in men (Bogin, 1988, 1993, 1994a).

## Mathematical evidence for childhood

Clearly, the human pattern of growth is qualitatively and quantitatively different from the pattern for other primates. The quantitative differences can be expressed in amounts, rates and timing of growth events, and are so reported in many standard textbooks of human growth (e.g. Tanner, 1962; Bogin, 1988). These quantitative differences may also be expressed in terms of the type and number of mathematical functions that are needed to describe growth. The distance and velocity curves for most mammalian species can be estimated by a single function, such as a simple polynomial or exponential function. Even the monkeys and apes, with the addition of the juvenile stage, require no more than two such relatively simple functions (Laird, 1967; Bogin, 1988: 57–60). The insertion of the mid-childhood and adolescent spurts into human ontogeny means that at least three mathematical functions are needed to adequately describe shape of the velocity curve (Figure 2.6). Not only more, but also more complex functions are needed. It is vitally important to stress here that all of this quantitative knowledge of the biology of human growth is well established and widely available. This information unequivocally negates neoteny, hypermorphosis or any other single heterochronic process as the primary cause of human evolution. Lamentably, the works on neoteny cited above – with the exception of Shea's work – make little or no reference to studies of the physical growth and development of living people.

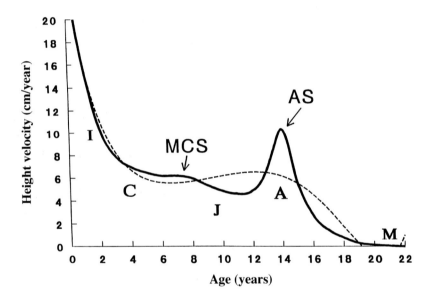

Figure 2.6. Idealised (see text) velocity curve of human growth for boys (———). I: infancy; C: childhood; J: juvenile; A: adolescence; M: mature adult. The dashed line is a sixth degree polynomial curve fit to the velocity curve data. The polynomial curve does not fit well to real growth data due to the pulses of the mid-childhood spurt (MCS) and the adolescent spurt (AS). The human velocity curve cannot be fitted adequately by a single continuous mathematical function. Two or more functions are required.

# How and when did the human pattern evolve?

The stages of the life cycle may be studied directly only for living species; however, there are lines of evidence on the life cycle of extinct species. Such inferences for the hominids are, of course, hypotheses based on comparative anatomy, comparative physiology, comparative ethology and archaeology. Examples of this methodology are found in the work of Martin (1983) and Harvey et al. (1987) on patterns of brain and body growth in apes, humans and their ancestors.

Apes have a pattern of brain growth that is rapid before birth and relatively slower after birth. In contrast, humans have rapid brain growth both before and after birth (Figure 2.7). This difference may be appreciated by comparing the ratios of brain weight divided by total body weight (in grams). At birth this ratio averages 0.09 for the great apes and 0.12 for human neonates. At adulthood the ratio averages 0.008 for the great apes and 0.028 for humans. In other words, relative to body size the human neonatal brain size is 1.33 times larger than the great apes, but by adulthood the difference is 3.5 times. The human–ape difference is not due to any single heterochronic process, i.e. not the result of delay, prolongation or acceleration of a basic ape-like pattern of growth. Rather, it is the result of new patterns of growth for the human species. The rate of human brain growth exceeds that of most other tissues of the body during the first few years after birth (Figure 2.5). Martin (1983) and Harvey et al. (1987) also show that human neonates have remarkably large brains (corrected for body size) compared with other primate species. Together, relatively large neonatal brain size and the high postnatal growth rate give adult humans the largest encephalisation quotient (an allometric scaling of brain to body size) of all higher primates (Figure 2.8).

Finally, Martin (1983) argues that a 'human-like' pattern of brain and body growth becomes necessary once adult hominid brain size reaches about 850 cc. This biological marker is based on an analysis of cephalo–pelvic dimensions of foetuses and their mothers across a wide range of social mammals, including cetaceans, extant primates and fossil hominids (Martin, 1983: 40–1). Given the mean rate of postnatal brain growth for living apes, an 850 cc adult brain

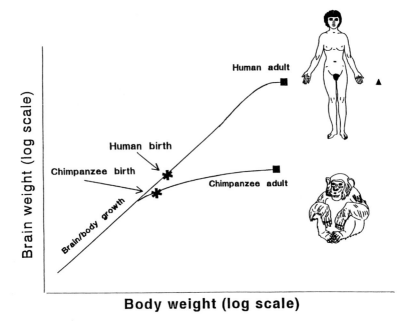

Figure 2.7. Growth curve for human brain and body compared with the chimpanzee. The length of the human foetal phase, in which brain and body grow at the same rate for both species, is extended for humans. Chimpanzee brain growth slows after birth, but humans maintain the high rate of brain growth during the postnatal phase. In contrast, the rate of human body growth slows after birth. If human brain/body growth rate were equal to the chimpanzee rate, then adult humans would weigh 454 kg and stand nearly 3.1 m tall (▲).

size may be achieved by all hominoids, including extinct hominids, by lengthening the foetal stage of growth. At brain sizes above 850 cc the size of the pelvic inlet of the fossil hominids, and living people, does not allow for sufficient foetal growth. Thus, a period of rapid postnatal brain growth and slow body growth – the human pattern – is needed to reach adult brain size.

Martin's analysis is elegant and tenable; nevertheless, the difference between ape and human brain growth is not only a matter of velocity, it is also a matter of life history stages. Brain growth for both apes and human beings ends at the start of the juvenile stage, which means that apes complete brain growth during infancy.

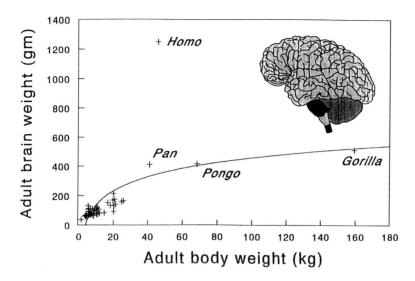

Figure 2.8. Adult body weight and brain weight plotted for 61 species of Cercopithecidae (Old world monkeys, apes and people). The curve is a logarithmic regression fit to the data for all species. The illustration is a sagittal section of the human brain. Each part of the human brain enlarged during evolution, especially the size of cerebral cortex.

Human beings, however, insert the childhood stage between the infant and juvenile stages. Childhood may provide the time and the continuation of parental investment necessary to grow the larger human brain. Following this line of reasoning, any fossil human, or any of our fossil hominid ancestors, with an adult brain size above Martin's 'cerebral Rubicon' of 850 cc may have included a childhood stage of growth as part of its life history.

Given this background, Figure 2.9 is my summary of the evolution of the human pattern of growth and development from birth to age 20 years (the evolution of adolescence is not discussed in this chapter, but see Bogin, 1993, 1994a; Bogin & Smith, 1996). Figure 2.9 must be considered as 'a work in progress' as only the data for the first and last species (*Pan* and *Homo sapiens*) are known with some certainty. The patterns of growth of the fossil hominid species are reconstructions based on published analyses of skeletal and dental development of fossil specimens that died before reaching adulthood.

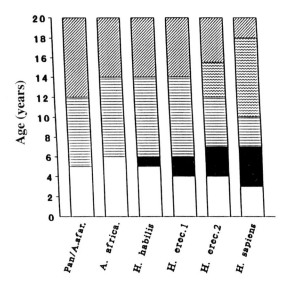

Figure 2.9. The evolution of hominid life history during the first 20 years of life: infancy (☐); childhood (■); juvenile (▤); adolescent (▦); adult (▨). Abbreviated nomenclature as follows: A. afar: *Australopithecus afarensis*; A. africa: *Australopithecus africanus*; H. habilis: *Homo habilis*; H. erec. 1: early *Homo erectus*; H. erec. 2: late *Homo erectus*; H. sapiens: *Homo sapiens*.

*Australopithecus afarensis* is a hominid, but shares many anatomical features with non-hominid species including an adult brain size of about 400 cc (Simons, 1989) and a pattern of dental development indistinguishable from extant apes (Smith, 1991b). The chimpanzee and *A. afarensis* are depicted in Figure 2.9, therefore, as sharing the typical tripartite stages of postnatal growth of social mammals: infant, juvenile, adult (Pereira and Fairbanks, 1993). To achieve the larger adult brain size of *A. africanus* (442 cc) may have required an addition to the length of infancy. The rapid expansion of adult brain size during the time of *Homo habilis* (650–800 cc) might have been achieved with expansion of both infancy and the juvenile period, as Martin's 'cerebral Rubicon' was not surpassed. The insertion of a brief childhood stage into hominid life history may have occurred. The archaeological evidence for intensification of stone tool manufacture and use to scavenge animal carcasses, especially bone marrow (Potts, 1988), may be interpreted as a strategy to feed children. Such scavenging may have been needed to provide the essential amino acids, some of the minerals and, especially, the fat (dense source of energy) that children require for growth of the brain and body (Leonard and Robertson, 1992).

Further brain size increase occurred during *H. erectus* times. The earliest adult specimens have brain sizes of 850–900 cc. This places *H. erectus* at or above Martin's 'cerebral Rubicon' and may justify an expansion of the childhood period to provide the high-quality foods needed for the rapid, human-like, pattern of brain growth. It should be noted from Figure 2.9 that from *Australopithecus* to *H. erectus*, the infancy period shrinks as the childhood stage expands. As will be discussed below, this gave *H. erectus*, and all later hominids, a reproductive advantage over all other hominoids. Later *H. erectus*, with adult brain sizes up to 1100 cc, are depicted with further expansions of childhood and the insertion of the adolescent stage. In addition to bigger brains, later *H. erectus* shows increased complexity of technology (tools, fire and shelter) and social organisation that were likely correlates of the biology and behaviour associated with further development of the childhood stage. The transition to archaic and finally modern *H. sapiens* expands the childhood stage to its current dimension.

## Who benefits from childhood?

Brain sizes of extant and fossil hominoids provide some idea of when human life stages may have evolved, but do not explain why they evolved. Bonner (1965) shows that the presence of a stage and its duration in the life cycle relate to such basic adaptations as locomotion, reproductive rates and food acquisition. To make sense out of the pattern of human growth one must look for the 'basic adaptations' that Bonner describes. The most basic of these adaptations are those that relate to evolutionary success. This is traditionally measured in terms of the number of offspring that survive and reproduce. As stated above, biological and behavioural traits do not evolve under the influence of natural selection unless they confer upon their owners some degree of reproductive advantage, in terms of survivors a generation or more later. Bogin (1988: 74–5) lists seven reasons for the evolution of human childhood from the perspective of reproductive success. The first three are the traditional 'textbook' explanations that emphasise learning, an idea that goes back to Spencer (1886), and even further back, to the dawn of written history, as social beliefs (Boyd, 1980). These three traditional explanations are that childhood provides for:

1. an extended period for brain growth,
2. time for the acquisition of technical skills, e.g. toolmaking and food processing, and
3. time for socialisation, play and the development of complex social roles and cultural behaviour.

These reasons are valid inasmuch they confer an advantage to pre-adult individuals. This brain-learning list of explanations, however, cannot account for the initial impetus for the insertion of childhood into human life history. A childhood stage of development is not necessary for the type of learning listed here. The prolonged infancy and juvenile period of the social carnivores (Bekoff and Beyers, 1985) and apes (Bogin, 1994b) can serve that function. Rather, childhood may be better viewed as a feeding and reproductive adaptation for the parents of the child as a strategy to minimise the risks of starvation and predation for the child, and as a mechanism that allows for more precise 'tracking' of ecological conditions via developmental plasticity during the growing years. These reproductive, survival and plasticity advantages of childhood are discussed, respectively, in the following sections.

## Human reproductive strategy

There are limits to amount of delay between birth and sexual maturity that any species can tolerate. The great apes are examples of this limit. Chimpanzee females in the wild reach menarche (the first menstruation) at 11–12 years of age and have their first births at an average age of 14 years (Goodall, 1983).

The average period between successful births in the wild is 5.6 years and young chimpanzees are dependent on their mothers for about 5 years (Teleki at al., 1976; Goodall, 1983; Nishida et al., 1990). Actuarial data collected on wild-living animals indicate that between 35% (Goodall, 1983) and 38% (Nishida et al., 1990) of all live-born chimpanzees survive to their mid-twenties. Although this is a significantly greater percentage of survival than for most other species of animals, the chimpanzee is at a reproductive threshold. Goodall (1983) reports that for the period 1965 to 1980 there were 51 births and 49 deaths in one community of wild chimpanzees at the Gombe Stream National Park, Tanzania. During a 10-year period at the Mahale Mountains National Park, Tanzania, Nishida et al. (1990) observed, '. . . 74 births, 74 deaths, 14 immigrations and 13 emigrations . . .' in one community. Chimpanzee population growth is, by these data, effectively equal to zero. Galdikas and Wood (1990) present data for the orang-utan which show that these apes are in a more precarious situation. Compared with the 5.6 years between successful births of chimpanzees, the orang-utan female waits 7.7 years, and orang-utan populations are in decline. Lovejoy (1981) calls the plight of great ape reproduction a 'demographic dilemma' (p. 211).

The great apes, and fossil hominids such as *Australopithecus* or early *Homo*, reached this demographic dilemma by extending infancy, forcing a demand on nursing to its limit (Figure 2.9). Extending infancy and birth intervals beyond the chimpanzee range was not possible if hominids such as *Homo habilis* were to remain extant. Our ancestors overcame the demographic dilemma by reducing the length of infancy and inserting childhood between the end of infancy and the juvenile period. Free from the demands of nursing and the physiological brake that nursing places on ovulation (Ellison, 1990), mothers could reproduce soon after their infants became children. This certainly occurs among modern humans. An often cited example, the !Kung, are a traditional hunting and gathering society of southern Africa. A !Kung woman's age at her first birth averages 19 years and as nursing lasts for 4 years subsequent births follow about every 3.6 years, resulting in an average fertility rate of 4.7 children per woman (Short, 1976; Howell, 1979). Women in another hunter–gatherer society, the Hadza (Blurton Jones et al., 1992), have even shorter intervals between successful births, stop nursing about 1 year earlier and average 6.15 births per woman.

These relationships are illustrated in Figure 2.10, a comparison of several life history events for female great apes and human beings. The data are drawn from studies of wild-living animals for the great apes and non-contracepting hunting and gathering or horticultural populations for human beings. The infancy dependency period for each of the apes species is longer than

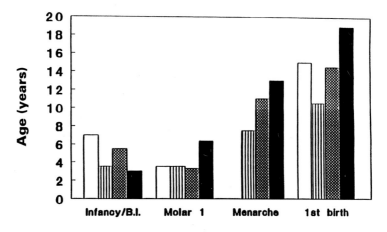

Figure 2.10. Hominoid developmental landmarks. Data based on observations of wild-living individuals or for humans, healthy individuals from various cultures. Note that compared with apes, people experience developmental delays in eruption of the first permanent molar, age at menarche and age at first birth. However, people have a shorter infancy and shorter birth interval (B.I.) which in apes and traditional human societies are virtually coincident. The net result is that humans have the potential for greater lifetime fertility than any ape. (□): *Pongo pygmaeus*; (Ⅲ): *Gorilla gorilla*; (▨): *Pan troglodytes*; (■): *Homo sapiens*. Developmental landmarks are: Infancy/B.I.: period of dependency on mother for survival, usually coincident with mean age at weaning and/or a new birth; molar 1: mean age at eruption of first permanent molar; menarche: mean age at first oestrus/menstrual bleeding; first birth: mean age of females at first offspring delivery. From Bogin and Smith (1996).

that for humans. Ape infancy ends after eruption of the first permanent molar, which is probably a requirement so that the juvenile ape can acquire and process foods of the adult diet (Smith, 1991a). Human infancy ends before eruption of the first permanent molar, i.e. before the youngster can process adult foods. The evolution of childhood as a stage in human life history 'fills the gap' between the infant's dependency on the mother for food via nursing and the feeding independence of the juvenile. The addition of a childhood stage and the prolongation of the juvenile and adolescent stages of development of humans also delays the age of both menarche and first birth. Compared with the great apes, however, humans reduce the birth spacing interval and, therefore, each woman may produce more offspring during her life than any female ape. This results in an increase in reproductive fitness if the additional offspring survive to maturity. !Kung, Hadza and all human parents help to ensure survival of their offspring by provisioning all their children with food, not just their current infant, for a decade or longer. The child must be given foods that are specially chosen and prepared and these may be provided by older juveniles, adolescents or adults. In Hazda society, for example, grandmothers and great-aunts are observed to supply a significant amount of food to children (Blurton Jones, 1993). In Agta society (Philippine hunter–gatherers) women hunt large game animals but still retain primary responsibility for child care. They accomplish this by living in extended family groups – two or three brothers and sisters, their spouses, children and parents – and sharing the child care (Estioko-Griffin, 1986). Among the Maya of Guatemala (horticulturalists and agriculturalists), many people live together in extended family compounds. Women of all ages work together in food preparation, manufacture of clothing and child care (Bogin, fieldwork notes, 1988–93). Juvenile girls associate with these working groups and the girls provide much of the direct care and feeding of children, but always under the guidance of adolescents and adults. In some societies fathers provide significant child care, including the Agta, who take their children on hunting trips, and the Aka Pygmies, a hunting–gathering people of central Africa (Hewlitt, 1991). Sum-marising the data from many human societies, Lancaster and Lancaster (1983) call this type of child care and feeding 'the hominid adaptation', for no other primate or mammal does this.

Given this unique behaviour of parents, grandparents, older sib-lings and other adults, it may be more profitable to view the advan-tages of childhood from the perspective of adults. This leads to the following five additional reasons for the evolution of childhood (these replace points 4 to 7 in Bogin, 1988: 75).

## Childhood is a feeding adaptation

A childhood growth stage may have originally evolved as a means by which the mother, the father and other kin could provision dependent offspring with food. This frees the mother from the demands of nursing and the inhibition of ovulation related to con-tinuous nursing. This decreases the interbirth interval and generally increases reproductive fitness.

Such provisioning, however, is effective only if older individuals provide foods appropriate to the needs of the child and, as well, feel compelled to meet these needs. Appropriate weaning foods are required because the small gastrointestinal tracts of young children are not capable of digesting sufficient quantities of the adult diet to meet all nutritional requirements, especially energy (Bogin, 1988: 130). This problem is alleviated in contemporary human societies by the selection of calorie-dense foods, as well as by using technology (e.g. tools and fire for cooking) to prepare weaning foods – behaviours first practised by *H. habilis* or early *H. erectus*. Alternatively, older individuals can provide adult-type foods that are partially predigested by mastication. These feeding strategies for children, however, require considerable investment of time and energy by the older individuals. A stimulus to release these behaviours towards children may be found in the very pattern of growth of the children themselves, in that:

## The allometry of the growth of the human child releases nurturing and care-giving behaviours in older individuals

The central nervous system, in particular the brain, follows a growth curve that is advanced over the curve for the body as a whole (Figure 2.5). The brain achieves adult size when body growth is only 40% complete, dental maturation is only 58% complete and reproductive maturation is only 10% complete. The allometry of the growth of the human child maintains an infantile appearance (large cranium, small face and body, little sexual development) which stimulates nurturing and care-giving behaviours in older individuals. A series of ethological observations (Lorenz, 1971) and psychological experiments (Todd et al., 1980; Alley, 1983) demonstrate that these growth patterns of body, face and brain allow the human child to maintain a superficially infantile (i.e. 'cute') appearance longer than any other mammalian species (Table 2.1 in Appendix). The infantile appearance of children facilitates parental investment by maintaining the potential for nurturing behaviour of older individuals towards both infants and dependent children (Bogin, 1988: 98–104; 1990; McCabe, 1988).

## Children are relatively inexpensive to feed

The relatively slow rate of body growth and small body size of children reduces competition with adults for food resources because slow-growing, small children require less total food than bigger individuals. A 5-year-old child of average size (the 50th centile of the NCHS reference curves for growth) and activity, for example, requires 22.7% less dietary energy per day for maintenance and growth than a 10-year-old juvenile on the 50th growth centile (Ulijaszek and Strickland, 1993; Guthrie and Picciano, 1995). Thus, provisioning children, though time consuming, is not as onerous a task of investment as it would be, for instance, if both brain and body growth were both progressing at the same rapid rate.

Similarly, the task of child care becomes even less onerous because:

### *'Babysitting' is possible*

As children do not require nursing, any competent member of a social group can provide food and care for them. Early neurological maturity versus late sexual maturity allows juveniles and young adolescents to provide much of their own care and also provide care for children (Bogin, 1994a). Grandmothers and other post-reproductive women also provide much child care. Again, this frees younger adults, especially the mother, for subsistence activity, adult social behaviours and further childbearing.

A further important reason for the evolution of childhood is that:

### *Childhood allows for developmental plasticity*

Following the discussion in Stearns (1992: 62), the term 'plasticity' means a change in the phenotype (physical appearance and behaviour) of the individual caused by a change in the environment. The fitness of a given phenotype varies across the range of variation of an environment. When phenotypes are fixed early in development, such as in mammals that mature sexually soon after weaning (e.g. rodents), environmental change and high mortality are positively correlated. Social mammals (carnivores, elephants, primates) prolong the developmental period by adding a juvenile stage between infancy and adulthood. Adult phenotypes develop more slowly in these mammals. They experience a wider range of environmental variation and the result is a better conformation between the individual and the environment. Fitness is increased in that more offspring survive to reproductive age than in mammalian species without a juvenile stage (Lancaster and Lancaster, 1983; Pereira and Fairbanks, 1993). Human beings insert the childhood stage between infancy and the juvenile period. This results in an additional 4 years of relatively slow physical growth and allows for behavioural experience that further enhances developmental plasticity. The combined result is increased fitness (reproductive success). By comparison, humans in traditional societies, such as hunters and gatherers and horticulturalists, rear about 50% of their live-born offspring to adulthood. Monkeys and apes rear between

12 and 36% of live-born offspring to adulthood. The initial human advantage may seem small, but it means that between 14 and 38 more people survive out of every 100 born – more than enough over the vast course of evolutionary time to make the evolution of human childhood an overwhelmingly beneficial adaptation.

## Conclusion

These five themes of childhood (feeding, nurturing, low cost, baby-sitting and plasticity) account for much of the evolution of and pattern of growth of our species. Understanding these themes helps to resolve the paradox of human growth and evolution: lengthy development and low fertility. In reality humans raise a greater percentage of offspring to adulthood than any other species. These successfully reared young adults then begin their own reproduction and thus ensure some 'intimation of immortality' for their parents. In the centre of it all is human childhood. For the child is indeed, to paraphrase Wordsworth, parent to the reproductively successful and well-adapted adult.

---

### APPENDIX:   THE EVOLUTIONARY PSYCHOLOGY OF CHILDHOOD

Reproductive success is the major force behind the evolution of all species. Part of the reproductive success of the human species is due to the intense investment and care that parents and other individuals lavish on infants and children. In the course of human evolution, at least since the appearance of the genus *Homo* in the last two million years, patterns of growth were shaped by natural selection to promote and enhance parental investment. One way this was accomplished was by stimulating what may be called the 'psychology of parenting'.

Lorenz (1971) stated that the physical characteristics of mammalian infants, including small body size, a relatively large head with little mandibular or nasal prognathism, relatively large round eyes in proportion to skull size, short thick extremities and clumsy movements, inhibit aggressive behaviour by adults and encourage their caretaking and nurturing behaviours. Lorenz believed that these infantile features trigger 'innate releasing mechanisms' in adult mammals, including humans, for the protection and care of dependent young. Gould (1979) questions the innateness of the human response to infantile features. Such behaviour may be '. . . learned from our immediate experience with babies and grafted upon an evolutionary predisposition for attaching ties of affection to certain learned signals' (p. 34). The important point is that whether innate or learned the resultant behaviour is the same.

There seems to be a pan-human ability to perceive the five stages of human postnatal development and respond appropriately to each. An elegant series of experiments performed by Todd et al. (1980) show that human perceptions of body shape and growth status are consistent between individuals. When adult subjects (about 40 college students, all childless) were shown a series of profiles of human skull proportions, they could easily arrange them correctly into a hierarchy spanning infancy to adulthood. The subjects could also ascribe maturity ratings to skull profiles that were geometrically transformed to imitate the actual changes that occur during growth (Figure 2.11). This perception was selective because a variety of other types of geometrical transformations elicited no reports of growth or maturation. When the growth-like mathematical transformations were applied to profile drawings of the heads of birds and dogs, human subjects reported identical perceptions of growth and maturation, even though in reality the development of these animals does not follow the human pattern of skull shape change. Even more surprising is that participants reported the perception of growth when the growth-like mathematical transformations were applied to front and side view profiles of Volkswagen 'beetles', objects which do not grow.

In another series of experiments, Alley (1983) studied the association between human body shape and size and the tendency by adults to protect and 'cuddle' other individuals. In the first experiment, subjects were shown two sets of drawings. One set was based upon two-dimensional diagrams depicting changes in human body proportion during growth. Alley's version of these diagrams are called 'shape-variant' drawings (Fig. 2.12(a)). Alley's second set of figures were called 'size-variant' drawings (Figure 2.12(b)). He used the middle-most, '6-year-old' profile in the shape-variant series to construct sets of figures that varied in height and width, but not in shape. Note that these figures have no facial features or genitals. Perceptual differences between figures are due to body shape or size alone.

The subjects of these experiments were 120 undergraduate students, 45 men and 75 women at an American university, whose ages ranged from 17 to 27 years (mean age 18.8 years). All subjects were childless and one-third had no younger siblings. For all experiments the subjects

*Cardioidal strain*

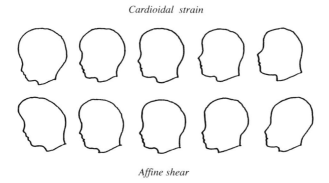

*Affine shear*

Figure 2.11. Two of the mathematical transformations of human head shape used in the experiments of Todd et al. (1980). The middle profile in each row was drawn from the photograph of a 10-year-old boy. The transformations were applied to this profile of a real child. The cardioidal strain transformation is perceived by most adults as growth. The affine shear transformation is not perceived as growth.

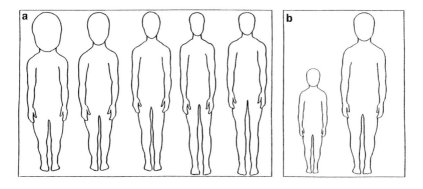

Figure 2.12. (a) The series of five shape-variant drawings used in the experiments of Alley (1983). These drawings show the typical body proportions of a male at (from left) birth, 2, 6, 12 and 25 years of age. (b) Example of the size-variant pairs of drawings used in the experiments of Alley (1983).

rated the drawings on a scale of 1 (low) to 9 (high). In the first experiment, the subjects were shown pairs of the shape-variant drawings (i.e. profiles of a newborn and a 6-year-old, a 2-year-old and a 12-year-old, etc.) or pairs of the size-variant drawings and asked to state which one of the pair they '. . . would feel most compelled to defend should you see them being beaten'. In another experiment they were asked about their feelings to 'hug or cuddle' the person depicted. The results of both experiments, summarized in Table 2.1, find a fairly strong reported willingness to defend 'newborns' and '2-year-olds', and a moderate willingness to defend 'older' persons. The reported willingness to cuddle decreased with the 'age' of the drawings. Placed in the context of the ethological study of 'parental' caregiving in mammals and birds, Alley believes that his results demonstrate a general tendency to protect or cuddle others based on the perception of maturational status.

McCabe (1988) reviews the work of Alley and other similar studies. Taken together, these studies indicate that adults are more likely to protect or nurture individuals with 'neotenous' facial features. McCabe defines such features as having a relatively large ratio of cranium size to lower face size. McCabe also cites studies of the facial features of nursery school-aged children under court protection for abuse compared with non-abused age-matched controls. The abused children had smaller ratios of the cranium/lower face, i.e. they were less 'neotenous' or 'cute', than the non-abused controls.

These psychological experiments and case-control studies provide support for the arguments developed in this chapter for the evolution of human childhood. In particular, small body size and a superficially infantile appearance promote appropriate parental behaviour by older individuals towards children.

Table 2.1. *Mean (and standard deviation) reported willingness to defend or cuddle persons of different body proportions*

| Age portrayed (years) | Defend | Cuddle |
|---|---|---|
| Newborn | 7.7 (1.7) | 3.4 (2.3) |
| 2 | 7.1 (1.7) | 3.4 (2.0) |
| 6 | 5.8 (1.8) | 3.2 (2.2) |
| 12 | 5.0 (1.9) | 3.0 (1.9) |
| 25 | 4.3 (1.9) | 2.7 (2.2) |

*Source:* from Alley (1983).

# References

Alley, T. R. (1983). Growth-produced changes in body shape and size as determinants of perceived age and adult caregiving. *Child Development*, **54**, 241–8.

Altmann, J. (1980). *Baboon Mothers and Infants*. Cambridge: Harvard University Press.

Bekoff, M. and Beyers, J. A. (1985). The development of behavior from evolutionary and ecological perspectives in mammals and birds. *Evolutionary Biology*, **19**, 215–86.

Bertalanffy, L. von. (1960). Principles and theory of growth. In: *Fundamental Aspects of Normal and Malignant Growth*, ed. W. N. Nowinski, pp. 137–259. Amsterdam: Elsevier.

Blurton Jones, N. G. (1993). The lives of hunter–gather children: effects of parental behavior and parental reproductive strategy. In: *Juvenile Primates*, ed. M. E. Pereira and L. A. Fairbanks, pp. 309–26. Oxford: Oxford University Press.

Blurton Jones, N. G., Smith, L. C., O'Connell, J. F and Handler, J. S. (1992). Demography of the Hadza, an increasing and high density population of savanna foragers. *American Journal of Physical Anthropology*, **89**, 159–81.

Bogin, B. (1988). *Patterns of Human Growth*. Cambridge: Cambridge University Press.

Bogin, B. (1990). The evolution of human childhood. *BioScience*, **40**, 16–25.

Bogin, B. (1993). Why must I be a teenager at all? *New Scientist*, **137**, 34–8.

Bogin, B. (1994a). Adolescence in evolutionary perspective. *Acta Paediatrica*, **406** (Suppl.), 29–35.

Bogin, B. (1994b). The evolution of learning. In: *The International Encyclopedia of Education* 2nd edn, ed. T. Husen and T. N. Postlethwaite, pp. 2681–5. Oxford: Pergamon Press.

Bogin, B. (1995). Growth and development: recent evolutionary and biocultural research. In: *Biological Anthropology: The State of the Science*, ed. N. Boaz and L. D. Wolfe, pp. 49–70. Bend, Oregon: International Institute for Human Evolutionary Research.

Bogin, B. (1996). Childhood in evolutionary and biocultural perspective. In: *Long Term Consequence of Early Environment*, ed. C. J. K. Kenry and S. J. Ulijaszek, pp. 7–22. Cambridge: Cambridge University Press.

Bogin, B. and Smith, B. H. (1996). Evolution of the human life cycle. *American Journal of Human Biology* (in press).

Bonner, J. T. (1965). *Size and Cycle*. Princeton, NJ: Princeton University Press.

Bowman, J. E. and Lee, P. C. (1995). Growth and threshold weaning weights among captive rhesus macaques. *American Journal of Physical Anthropology*, **96**, 159–75.

Boyd, E. (1980). *Origins of the Study of Human Growth*, ed. B. S. Savara and J. F. Schilke. Eugene: University of Oregon Health Sciences Center, Dental School.

Brody, S. (1945). *Bioenergetics and Growth*. New York: Reinhold Publishing Co.

Cabana, T., Jolicoeur, P. and Michaud, J. (1993). Prenatal and postnatal growth and allometry of stature, head circumference, and brain weight in Québec children. *Americna Journal of Human Biology*, **5**, 93–9.

Coelho, A. M. (1985). Baboon dimorphism: growth in weight, length and adiposity from birth to 8 years of age. In: *Nonhuman Primate Models for Human Growth*, ed. E. S. Watts, pp. 125–59. New York: Alan R. Liss.

Demirjian, A. (1978). Dentition. In: *Human Growth 2: Postnatal Growth*, ed. F. Falkner and J. M. Tanner, pp. 413–44. New York: Plenum.

Dettwyler, K. A. (1995). A time to wean: the hominid blueprint for the natural age of weaning in modern human populations. In: *Breastfeeding: Biocultural Perspectives*, ed. P. Stuart-Macadam and K. A. Dettwyler, pp. 39–73. New York: Aldine de Gruyter.

Ellison, P. T. (1990). Human ovarian function and reproductive ecology: new hypotheses. *American Anthropologist*, **92**, 933–52.

Estioko-Griffin, A. (1986). Daughters of the forest. *Natural History*, **95**, 36–43.

Galdikas, B. M. and Wood, J. W. (1990). Birth spacing patterns in humans and apes. *American Journal of Physical Anthropology*, **83**, 185–91.

Goodall, J. (1983). Population dynamics during a 15 year period in one community of free-living chimpanzees in the Tombe National Park, Tanzania. *Zeitschrift für Tierpsychologie*, **61**, 1–60.

Gould, S. J. (1977). *Ontogeny and Phylogeny*. Cambridge, Massachusetts: Belknap Press.

Gould, S. J. (1979). Mickey Mouse meets Konrad Lorenz. *Natural History*, **88**, 30–6.

Gould, S. J. (1981). *The Mismeasure of Man*. New York: Norton.

Guthrie, H. and Picciano, M. F. (1995). *Human Nutrition*. St Louis: Mosby.

Harvey, P. H., Martin, R. D. and Clutton-Brock, T. H. (1987). Life histories in comparative perspective. In: *Primate Societies*, ed. B. B. Smuts, D. L. Cheney, R. M. Seyfarth, R. W. Wrangham and T. T. Struhsaker, pp. 181–96. Chicago: University of Chicago Press.

Hewlitt, B. S. (1991). *Intimate Fathers: The Nature and Context of Aka Pygmy Paternal Care*. Ann Arbor, MI: University of Michigan Press.

Howell, N. (1979). *Demography of the Dobe !Kung*. New York: Academic Press.

Jaswal, S. (1983). Age and sequence of permanent tooth emergence among Khasis. *American Journal of Physical Anthropology*, **62**, 177–86.

Jolly, A. (1985). *The Evolution of Primate Behavior*, 2nd edn. New York: Macmillan.

Laird, A. K. (1967). Evolution of the human growth curve. *Growth*, **31**, 345–55.

Lancaster, J. B. and Lancaster, C. S. (1983). Parental investment: the hominid adaptation. In: *How Humans Adapt*, ed. D. J. Ortner, pp. 33–65. Washington, DC: Smithsonian Institution Press.

Lee, P. C., Majluf, P. and Gordon, I. J. (1991). Growth, weaning and maternal investment from a comparative perspective. *Journal of the Zoological Society of London*, **225**, 99–114.

Leonard, W. R. and Robertson, M. L. (1992). Nutritional requirements and human evolution: a bioenergetics model. *American Journal of Human Biology*, **4**, 179–95.

Lorenz, K. (1971). Part and parcel in animal and human societies: a methodological discussion. In: *Studies in Animal and Human Behavior*, vol. 2, ed. and trans. R. Martin, pp. 115–95. Cambridge: Harvard University Press.

Lovejoy, C. O. (1981). The origin of man. *Science*, **211**, 341–50.

Martin, R. D. (1983). *Human brain evolution in an ecological context*. Fifty-second James Arthur Lecture. New York: American Museum of Natural History.

McCabe, V. (1988). Facial proportions, perceived age, and caregiving. In: *Social and Applied Aspects of Perceiving Faces*, ed. T. R. Alley, pp. 89–95. Hillsdale, NJ: Lawrence Erlbaum Associates.

McKinney, M. L. and McNamara, K. J. (1991). *Heterochrony: The Evolution of Ontogeny*. New York: Plenum Press.

Nishida, T., Takasaki, H. and Takahata, Y. (1990). Demography and reproductive profiles. In: *The Chimpanzees of the Mahale Mountains: Sexual and Life History Strategies*, ed. T. Nishida, pp. 63–97. Tokyo: University of Tokyo Press.

Parker, S. T. (1996). Using cladistic analysis of comparative data to reconstruct the evolution of cognitive development in hominids. In: *Phylogenies and the Comparative Method in Animal Behavior*, ed. E Martins, pp. 443–8. Oxford: Oxford Univresity Press.

Pereira, M. E. and Altmann, J. (1985). Development of social behavior in free-living nonhuman primates. In: *Nonhuman Primate Models for Human Growth and Development*, ed. E. S. Watts, pp. 217–309. New York: Alan R. Liss.

Pereira, M. E. and Fairbanks, L. A. (eds). (1993). *Juvenile Primates*. Oxford: Oxford University Press.

Piaget, J. and Inhelder, B. (1969). *The Psychology of the Child*. New York: Basic Books.

Potts, R. (1988). *Early Hominid Activities at Olduvai*. New York: Aldine de Gruyter.

Scammon, R. E. (1930). The measurement of the body in childhood. In: *The Measurement of Man*, ed. J. A. Harris, C. M. Jackson, D. G. Paterson and R. E. Scammon, pp. 173–215. Minneapolis: University of Minnesota Press.

Shea, B. T. (1989). Heterochrony in human evolution: the case for neoteny reconsidered. *Yearbook of Physical Anthropology*, **32**, 69–101.

Short, R. V. (1976). The evolution of human reproduction. *Proceedings, Royal Society*, Series B, **195**, 3–24.

Simons, E. L. (1989). Human origins. *Science*, **245**, 1343–50.

Smith, B. H. (1991a). Age at weaning approximate age of emergence of the first permanent molar in non-human primates. *American Journal of Physical Anthropology*, **12** (Suppl.), 163–4 (abstract).

Smith, B. H. (1991b). Dental development and the evolution of life history in Hominidae. *American Journal of Physical Anthropology*, **85**, 157–74.

Smith, B. H. (1992). Life history and the evolution of human maturation. *Evolutionary Anthropology*, **1**, 134–42.

Smith, B. H., Crummett, T. L. and Brandt, K. L. (1994). Ages of eruption of primate teeth: a compendium for aging individuals and comparing life histories. *Yearbook of Physical Anthropology*, **37**, 177–231.

Spencer, H. (1886). *The Principles of Biology*, vols I and II. New York: D. Appleton.

Stearns, S. C. (1992). *The Evolution of Life Histories*. Oxford: Oxford University Press.

Tanner, J. M. (1947). The morphological level of personality. *Proceedings of the Royal Society of Medicine*, **40**, 301–3.

Tanner, J. M. (1962). *Growth at Adolescence*, 2nd edn. Oxford: Blackwell Scientific Publications.

Tanner, J. M., Wilson, M. E. and Rudman, C. G. (1990). Pubertal growth spurt in the female Rhesus monkey: relation to menarche and skeletal maturation. *American Journal of Human Biology*, **2**, 101–6.

Teleki, G. E., Hunt, E. and Pfifferling, J. H. (1976). Demographic observations (1963–1973) on the chimpanzees of the Gombe National Park, Tanzania. *Journal of Human Evolution*, **5**, 559–98.

Todd, J. T., Mark, L. S., Shaw, R. E. and Pittenger, J. B. (1980). The perception of human growth. *Scientific American*, **242**, 132–44.

Ulijaszek, S. J. and Strickland, S. S. (1993). *Nutritional Anthropology: Prospects and Perspectives*. London: Smith Gordon.

Vrba, E. S. (1996). Climate, heterochrony and human evolution. *Journal of Anthropological Research*, **52**, 1>EN-28.

Weisner, T. S. (1987). Socialization for parenthood in sibling caretaking societies. In: *Parenting Across the Life Span: Biosocial Dimensions*, ed. J. B. Lancaster, J. Altmann, A. S. Rossi and L. R. Sherrod, pp. 237–70. New York: Aldine de Gruyter.

# 3

## From the child's point of view: issues in the social construction of childhood

ALLISON JAMES

## Introduction

The suggestion that childhood is a social construction may seem to be yet another example of the post-modern gone mad within contemporary social science; to suggest, as Phillipe Ariès (1979 [1962]) did, that childhood was invented may seem to some to have gone just too far! Yet, as this chapter argues, it was precisely this provocative suggestion which stimulated a flurry of activity in childhood studies within the social sciences during the 1970s. It is one which, by now, is yielding a rich and varied body of theoretical and ethnographic accounts of childhood through cross-cultural research with children. The intention in this chapter is to outline the main themes of this debate, assess its impact and to illustrate its importance for contemporary sociological and anthropological work on childhood. Three key research issues are examined: first, the idea that childhood is a social and cultural, rather than universal, phenomenon; second, the recognition of the importance of children's own experiences for any understanding of childhood; and third, the value which this 'new paradigm' for childhood study has for a contemporary understanding of children's lives (Prout and James, 1990).

## Childhood as a cultural universal?

It is the work of the French historian Phillipe Ariès which is conventionally taken as the starting point for the new sociological approaches to childhood, for it was his radical suggestion that in mediaeval society childhood did not exist which unleashed a stream of questions about the nature and universality of childhood. In brief, Ariès' suggestion was that although children – in the form of younger members of the species – clearly existed in mediaeval times, the attention and thought given to them, once weaned, was just as people. They were for the most part much like adults and were not granted special or distinctive status; nor were they accorded that difference in kind which, as Jenks (1982) has remarked, is emblematic of contemporary Western childhood. Ariès' task, as he saw it, was to document how that shift in percep- tion produced the modern conceptions of children and childhood now recognised in contemporary Western societies. Caricatured by Holt, these Western children are 'a mixture of expensive nuisance, fragile treasure, slave and super-pet' and childhood a 'kind of walled garden in which children, being small and weak, are pro- tected from the harshness of the world outside until they become strong and clever enough to cope with it' (Holt, 1975: 22).

In focusing on the institution of childhood, rather than on atti- tudes towards children, Ariès was at pains to note that his was not a history of sensibility. Rather, it was an account of the ways in which childhood, as a particular social formation, became insti- tutionalised for boys, and later for girls, through specific changes in legal, social and educational spheres. The absence of the social institution of 'childhood' and thus of 'the child' as a status category in earlier times, he argued, was not therefore to be regarded as a sign of barbarity (parental affection and love for children were unequivocally present) but, instead, was to be taken as evidence of an insensibility to the idea that children might require a different and specific kind of social experience. According to Ariès this meant that within the mediaeval world view, once past infancy, children's needs were seen to be no different from those of adults. Thus, it is the gradual institutionalisation of specifically children's needs which, for Ariès, marks the beginnings of 'childhood'. As Jenks puts it, 'the child emerges in contemporary culture as a formal category and as a social status accompanied by programmes of care and schemes of education' (Jenks, 1988: 11).

There have, however, been a number of objections to Ariès' thesis, most of which centre on the historical accuracy and detail of his claims (Fuller, 1979; Wilson, 1980; Shahar, 1990). Pollock's (1983) critique is based on an analysis of primary sources between 1500 and 1900 and is one of the more influential. She argues that there is little evidence to support the view that childhood is a modern invention; differences between adults and children have always been acknowledged, although exactly how those differences are conceptualised and constituted *does* change over time. Thus, although Pollock is critical of Ariès' historiography, her more modest acknowledgement of childhood change lends support to the broad thrust of his reasoning: in sum, the institution of 'childhood' – how children are regarded, how they are treated and expectations about their competencies and abilities as social actors – varies both over time and in social space. Indeed, it was precisely this observation that writers within the culture and personality school of social anthropology had demonstrated some years earlier (see, for example, Mead and Wolfenstein, 1955). It was, then, the realisation that the biological 'facts of nature' are subject to different interpretations within cultures which provided the springboard for what amounted to a new wave of interest in the study of childhood.

## Envisioning the child

One of the major challeges which this social constructionist approach made was to the conventional accounts of child development offered by developmental psychology. Hitherto this had been the paramount discourse within which child study had taken place (Prout and James, 1990; Jenks, 1996b). Now that 'childhood' could no longer be regarded as a universal and unvarying experience for all children and now that expectations about the abilities and competencies of 'the child' had been shown to vary cross-culturally and over time, it was suggested that biological development must be seen as contextualising, rather than unequivocally determining, children's experiences. Thus, researchers across the social sciences, and including developmental psychologists themselves (see, for example, Richards and Light, 1986; Stainton-Rogers, 1989), began to explore the import of a social constructionist perspective both in theory and for practice. Dunn (1986), for example, in an early critical review of John Bowlby's model of mother–child attachment, argued against its universalising implications by stressing the importance of different family environments in shaping children's affective relationships and processes of cognition. Similarly, both Light (1986) and Walkerdine (1988) questioned the universal value of test results gained via the traditional experimental methods of developmental psychology. They argued, convincingly, that the social context of the experiment shaped children's responses due to the different knowledges possessed by children and adult researchers and their relative positions of power. Such social factors, they argued, affect the reliability of experiments and thus cast grave doubts on some of developmental psychology's more universalising and widely accepted claims about children's cognitive abilities. Also, more recently, from a cross-cultural perspective Woodhead has used a social constructionist approach to argue that any child development programmes must take account of the 'very different social and cultural assumptions, values and goals for childhood' which are espoused within local settings, rather than assuming that child development is culture free (Woodhead, 1996: 87). In Trinidad and Tobago, for example, the achievement of language and motor skills may be given less priority than a child's spiritual development. To be successful, then, any child development programme must take note of its cultural bias.

Within sociology and anthropology social constructionist approaches have adopted a broader remit and have charted the ways in which ideas or discourses of 'the child' are envisioned for children through the social institution of childhood. A first concern has been to explore the historical symbolisation of 'the child' which, in Western societies, for example, has worked to mythologise childhood through ideas of otherness, naturalness, innocence and a vulnerable dependence (Hockey and James, 1993). Accompanied by shifts in the affective positioning of children (DeMause, 1976;

Boswell, 1988), it was out of such discourses that modern Western childhood emerged:

> the extant vision of childhood through the nineteenth and twentieth century has become one of 'futurity', and the much vaunted accretion of a 'caring', 'helping', 'enabling', 'facilitating' mode of nurture instances the explicit awakening of a collective attitude more sensitive to children's needs, but also an implicit recognition of their worth and appropriate usage.
>
> (Jenks, 1996a: 15)

Thus, Jenks argues, what can be seen emerging over time is a growing sensitivity to the idea that children, being different from adults, require special treatment and care and that the importance of children lies in the future which they represent. In sum, children are to be nurtured and cherished in their potential as the next generation of adults. Such a view, he suggests, accounts for another salient feature of this emerging perspective on childhood: the need to separate children off from the dangerous adult world, and to seclude them in a distinctive social and cultural world of childhood. Through this the future which children represent might be better protected. This view Jenks finds reflected in changes in attitudes towards children's welfare:

> The apparent gradual diminution of child abuse through the nineteenth century and on into the twentieth century can be seen as a considered shift from immediate to deferred gratification on the part of an increasingly enlightened adult society.
>
> (Jenks, 1996a: 15)

The idea that a specific form of training, combined with a caring and enabling environment, is fundamental to sustaining a vision of children as the 'next generation' belies the extent to which such 'needs' are, as developmental psychologists now readily acknowledge, cultural as well as simply biological (Woodhead, 1990).

Another body of sociological and anthropological work has similarly been concerned to explore the diversity of childhoods through a focus on the cultural construction of childhood. This work, however, charts differences across space rather than time and explores the wide variety of ideas about 'the child' to be found expressed in child-rearing practices cross-culturally. In many cases the vision of the protected and innocent child, so characteristic of Western childhood (Ennew, 1986), is almost entirely absent. Among the Inuit of the Arctic circle, for example, the idea of the child as futurity – as the next generation of adults – is engendered through radically different means. As Briggs points out, child rearing is aimed at teaching children some of the harsh realities of life for the Canadian Inuit:

> [Inuit children] can't sit back comfortably, passively absorb the fruits of adult wisdom and experience and conclude that this wisdom embodies final and permanent answers. Instead of learning to depend passively on 'authorities' and 'experts' they learn to rely on their own sense in interpreting their own experience, to be watchful, doubtful, alert to hidden meanings and intentions and to keep testing others, as the adults have tested them.
>
> (Briggs, 1990: 38)

Through the seemingly harsh games which adults play with their children – games which teasingly threaten that a child's mother might die or hint at the child's own mortality – children are taught to be observant of the world around them. These lessons are for the future when, as adults, they must survive the precariousness of Inuit life. Thus, the Inuit understanding of 'the child' is not as a dependent incompetent but is, instead, respectful of 'the ability of three-year-olds to understand and to use in their own lives, emotionally complicated and difficult lessons' (Briggs, 1990: 38).

Hendry's (1986) work on Japanese childhood reveals yet another vision of what childhood might entail. The stress upon protection and childhood happiness, which Ennew notes as characteristic of Western childhood, becomes subtly translated within the Japanese context. Hendry notes that whereas young British and American children might have their fears assuaged by words of comfort from their parents through reassurances that dangers do not exist, Japanese children are made well aware of dangers and threats, but at the same time are assured of parental protection:

> In general, the encouragement of fear, and eventually courage, seems
> to be quite an important part of child training. The word for 'danger'
> (*abunai*) is used a great deal by adults with small children, as I learned
> first of all by having to translate it endlessly before my own children
> could understand any Japanese. I noticed then that in English we
> would be much more likely to use the positive phrase 'be careful' than
> the negative one 'that's dangerous'. In the country, some old people
> went further, specially at night, and pointed down dark alleyways
> suggesting that there might be a ghost or a big dog lurking there, so
> that the child should remain close to the safety of the adult's side.
>
> (Hendry, 1986: 113)

Thus, the innocence, and often ignorance, fostered through British
and American ideologies of childhood are not thought an essential
or 'natural' part of the Japanese child's experience of childhood.

Field's work takes these observations on Japanese childhood
further, arguing that the Japanese educational system is far
removed from the enabling, child-centred ideologies current within
contemporary British educational thinking. Taking up Postman's
(1982) argument that 'childhood' is effectively disappearing in the
late twentieth century through the technological revolution which
enables learning to take place at a rapid pace, Field describes how
Japanese children 'are suffering and risking the loss of childhood
itself precisely by performing the socially defined tasks of childhood'
(Field, 1995: 53). The rigours of a strict disciplinary regimen, high
degrees of competitiveness, long and arduous hours, a work pattern
dictated by the school system and encouraged by mothers focused
on their children's future success means, Field argues, that there is
a 'new continuity between childhood and adulthood' (Field, 1995:
68). Children, like their adult counterparts, are envisioned as productive labourers for the nation state; they are not accorded a different treatment just because they are children. In this sense, in
contemporary Japan, 'the child' is no longer characterised by 'difference and particularity' (Jenks, 1982: 10).

It is, then, precisely through such alarms about the disappearance of childhood that its socially constructed character is most
fully revealed; if 'childhood' were simply and unproblematically a
description of the early biological development of the human child,
then such discussions would be nonsensical. Children as younger

members of the species have existed and will always exist. It is the attribution of particular characteristics to them, characteristics which, as Holt (1975) notes, usually emphasise their inabilities as latent adults, rather than their particular abilities as children, which changes over time and which is subject to cultural variation.

It is ironic, therefore, that one of the problems brought to light by the Declaration of the Rights of the Child, which aimed to ensure a global set of children's rights – based in large part on Western conceptions of what children 'need' *because they are children* – is the near impossibility of drawing up universal criteria for children's rights, for the conceptualisation of those 'needs' are subject to massive cultural variability. While the rights to equality, regardless of race, religion, nationality or sex or the right to a name and a nationality might seem to be uncontroversial, other rights are far more problematic for, as Boyden notes, they embody a particular idea of childhood. The consequences for children of its globalisation may, therefore, be potentially disastrous. For example, the right to education, though humanitarian, may in practice work to further penalise the children of the poor in developing countries through placing the burden of paying for education upon their families: 'schooling for many children acts neither as a channel for upward social mobility nor as an instrument of social change and personal development but as yet another medium of social control' (Boyden, 1990: 208). Thus, one of the achievements of social constructionist approaches is a recognition that the articulation of children's rights from within a framework of childhood universals which are determined in large part by the biological and psychological facts of cognitive and biological development, may work to disempower children through the inappropriate globalisation of a Western model of childhood (Burman, 1994).

## Childen as social actors

The second key contribution to current debates about the social construction of childhood (Jenks, 1982; James and Prout, 1990) also has its roots in the 1970s. It derives from Charlotte Hardman's suggestion that the study of childhood need no longer simply be the adult study of children's socialisation or child development. Children themselves, she argued, are capable and key informants about childhood. Noting the vast collection of the lore, language and games of children gathered together by the Opies (1959, 1969), which reveals considerable continuity in form and style across both time and space, Hardman argued that children might be seen as possessing their own culture: 'an autonomous world which does not necessarily reflect early development of adult culture' (Hardman, 1973: 87). Thus, she argued, if adults wish to know what childhood is like then children should be studied 'in their own right and not just as receptacles of adult teaching' (Hardman, 1973: 87).

Here was a different perspective on childhood indeed and one which, though not explicitly linked at that time to the emerging social constructionist view of childhood, certainly fanned the flames of the argument. No longer were children simply to be regarded as passive objects to be shaped into adult members of society, such that success meant socialisation and failure an unwanted deviance. For Hardman, such traditional approaches denied children's own part in processes of cultural learning, for they,

> see the child as continually assimilating, learning and responding to the adult, having little autonomy, contributing nothing to social values or behaviour except the latent outpourings of earlier acquired experiences. The adult plays the role of either frustrating the child in its toilet training, feeding or other activities, or compelling children to fit to a cultural pattern.
>
> (Hardman, 1973: 87)

To understand 'childhood', in Hardman's view, we should ask children themselves. This was a simple but fundamental point.

Fundamental, that is, because what it suggested was that child thinking might be 'interesting in its own right' (Hardman, 1973: 86). Perhaps, more importantly, it also challenged the 'incompetence' model of traditional child development through the suggestion that children could be regarded as independent and reliable informants about the social world and that they could be as articulate as adults. It is a suggestion which has by now become central to the key debates in both academic and policy arenas. A growing body of academic work, for example, explores children's perspectives on a wide range of issues: the experience of work (Nieuwenhuys, 1994), surgery and hospitalisation (Bluebond-Langner, 1978; Alderson, 1993) health care (Mayall, 1996) and schooling (Davies, 1982; Pollard, 1985; Pollard and Filer, 1996).

Underpinning some of this work is the political agenda of children's rights (Archard, 1993), rights to humanitarian treatment which, for many children, include the right not to be treated simply as incompetent. One fundamental issue, therefore, is simply children's right to be heard and listened to and not to be, as they have for so long, a 'muted group' in Western societies (Hardman, 1973). Here, then, is the fusing of the theoretical issues raised by social constructionism and the call for children to be regarded as independent social actors: once the universalising developmental framework surrounding childhood was challenged, the status of children's accounts, and their right to be taken account of, could no longer be questioned through reference to their supposed lack of cognitive ability. The social circumstances of children had to be acknowledged.

Taking up this challenge to see the world as children do, Bluebond-Langner's (1978) work among children with leukemia in North America was one of the earliest ethnographic studies of children's lives. In her account of the dying worlds of children she details the different ways in which young children got to know their own prognosis and that of other children on the ward. Through a symbolic reading of forms of treatment and styles of adult behaviour towards them, the children gained knowledge about their illness and also learnt how to shield adults (parents and nursing staff) from the knowledge of their awareness. In the children's view it was better that adults should not know; the children believed that adults wished them to retain their childhood innocence. In a similar way Alderson's (1993) work on children's consent to surgery demonstrates how images of what childhood *should be* are employed by adults (parents and clinicians) to deny or obviate children's rights to take decisions. Focusing on a group of British children undergoing painful, lengthy and often experimental, orthopaedic surgery, Alderson's study shows how many children find themselves caught in a double-bind: if they exert their right to speak, but take a decision which adults regard as ill considered, then that decision-making risks being disregarded as merely evidence of children's lack of ability to reach informed consent:

> the main reason for denying rights to children is the assumption that children are foolish and respecting their autonomy will sabotage their rights to necessary resources and protection. 'Give them a choice and of course they won't have their operation or go to school' are typical arguments. Women were similarly regarded not too long ago.
>
> (Alderson, 1993: 40)

Another important set of issues to arise out of the suggestion that children can be regarded as articulate and competent social actors, with their own views on and about the social world, centres more directly on the claim from social constructionism that children's experiences of childhood might not just be determined by the immaturity of their minds and bodies. If, following Hardman and others, children could be said to have a 'culture', which is different from that of adults, then it is but a simple step to argue that children in different parts of the globe might conceivably have different child cultures; however, the ethnographic studies of childhood which followed in the wake of Hardman's suggestion were mostly studies of childhood within Western societies. This has meant that there is, as yet, still insufficient cross-cultural material to assess whether semi-autonomous children's cultures such as those depicted by James (1979, 1993) and Thorne (1993), for Britain and the USA, respectively, are to be found elsewhere. What child-focused studies there are seem, though, to imply the opposite: that children's and adults' worlds are *less* socially divided and culturally distinguished in contexts outside the USA and Western Europe. This suggests, then, that the image of childhood as representing a different, even 'natural' children's world, one of the redolent images by which Western childhood is characterised, may be a perception of children's lives unheard of elsewhere. It is but one cultural construction of the early period of human life.

Recent policy-focused research on children illustrates, for example, the cultural luxury which such a view of 'childhood' entails and suggests that it is neither inevitable, necessary nor, perhaps, even desirable. In developing countries a focus on children as social actors has revealed the relative absence of 'childhood' as a particular and distinctive social phase in the life course (Johnson et al., 1995; Save the Children, 1995). Instead, children are more often depicted in more adult-like roles: as contributors to family income through wage labour and agriculture, as domestic workers, as carers, as soldier, as sex workers and political activists (Stephens, 1995). In short, they are depicted as fully participating members of an adult, not a child, community:

> We know of a group of community workers who know every inch of the village in which they work, who are accepted by everyone, who want to help their community, who will work hard (for short periods of time) and cheerfully (all the time). Last month the health worker asked them to collect information about which children had been vaccinated in the village. Next Tuesday some of them will help remind the villagers that the baby clinic is coming and they will be at hand to play with the older children when mothers take their babies to see the nurse. Next month they plan to help the school teacher in a village clean-up campaign. These health workers are the boys and girls of the village.
>
> (Hawes and Scotchmer, cited in Save the Children, 1995: 36)

A similar picture emerges in Reynolds' study of healers in Zimbabwe where, she notes, children participate in the adult world in ways which, albeit may be less intense, are not seen as actions of a very different or inferior kind. Children's dreams may be read, at the age of six or seven, as signs of the child's possession by a spirit and indicative of their potential as a healer in the future. Such children will then begin to acquire healing knowledge by working alongside adult healers, who are often also family members:

> As technical knowledge is not taught but revealed, it is no use teaching a child how to identify plants, classify species, prepare 'medicines' and so on unless the child is guided at least by a *shave* [spirit]. Without spiritual guidance the child will simply forget. Therefore, a child with a quick, agile, interested mind that holds information and acquires more will be seen to be spiritually guided.

In attaching herself to a healer within the family and in offering her company, doing as bidden, and assisting with the collection of herbs and preparation of medicines, the child is declaring herself to be in communication with the supernatural.

(Reynolds, 1996: 38)

In other studies we get further glimpses of how variable is the idea of 'the child' cross-culturally. Among the Chewong of the Malay peninsula children are denied human status until reaching maturity (Howell, 1987), while, to return to an earlier example, for the Inuit maturity is thought to be evidenced in the appearance of *isuma*. Roughly translated as 'consciousness, thought, reason, memory, will' (Briggs, 1986: 5) it is something which grows naturally, as does the child. It cannot be inculcated through scolding but becomes visible through the child demonstrating a willingness to learn. Among the Zezuru people of Zimbabwe a child is innocent and yet this does not relieve them of social responsibility as it does, for example, British children who can seek protection of the law for misdemeanours committed under the age of 10 years old (James and Jenks, 1996). Reynolds writes:

For Zezuru, children are pure: they represent non evil. They belong to the shades. Their innocence does not imply a state of passivity. Rather children's own resources are bolstered by the protection afforded by living and dead kin. This is different from a notion of children as innocents who are corruptible and therefore in need of control . . . Children are from an early age seen to be responsible for their actions . . . Children are active in shaping their ascribed positions, forming identities for themselves that may even redefine others' perceptions of their assigned places within the community.

(Reynolds, 1996: 71)

From such examples it is clear, then, that what a child-centred approach to be the study of children's lives has achieved is a radically changed focus on 'childhood'. It has allowed us, for example, to see what the world looks like through children's rather than adults' eyes as Connolly and Ennew show in their discussion of risk and children's use of the environment:

located at the heart of the urban system [the city streets] offer a number of consumer and entertainment possibilities: fast food outlets,

restaurants, gambling arcades, cinemas and video stores, all with easy
transport access. For young people these attractions are multiplied by
the apparent lack of structure and schedule in these areas.

(Connolly and Ennew, 1996: 134)

In thus making children's voices audible, a child-centred approach
has therefore further defused the persuasive power of a dominant
perspective on children's needs which is decontextualised. It is now
possible to see, for example, that the 'problem' of children's physical and psychological welfare in developing contexts cannot simply
be solved by 'simplistic solutions, such as banning all child labour'
and placing these children, like their Western counterparts, in a
position of social, emotional and physical dependency (Johnson et
al., 1995: 2). In ignoring the socially constructed character of childhood, through promulgating a culturally specific version, such an
approach can have potentially devastating consequences for children. First, it ignores the fact that in Peru, for example, 'national
census records have shown that many 6- to 14-year-olds are actually heads of households and the principal wage earners' (Johnson
et al., 1995: 5). To remove children from the labour force would
simply exacerbate their poverty. Second, such an approach assumes
that exclusion from the adult world and seclusion in a child's world
will necessarily be of benefit. As Ennew (1995) notes, at least on
epistemological, if not practical, grounds, such an assumption must
be questioned:

> Children are a unique reminder of the past and signals of the future.
> In all societies, children represent the possibility of continuing all that
> is best and achieving all that is yearned for. This is as it should be.
> However, all too often children are treated as human beings on
> probation. Innovative participation on their part is discouraged in
> favour of socialisation into facsimiles of the adults around them. They
> thus become bearers of all the mistakes of both past and present.
>
> (Cited in Johnson et al., 1995: 6)

## Children's construction of childhood

In tracing out the background to the contemporary sociological
and anthropological discussions of childhood which have emerged

out of social constructionism, so far, this chapter has made three claims: first that childhood – the social experience of being a young person in society – cannot be regarded as universal for this varies from culture to culture; second, that if the socially constructed character of childhood is acknowledged, the extent to which psychological, if not physical, determinants on children's actions can or should be regarded as universal is also brought into question: are they not perhaps better regarded as constraints on children's actions which must be culturally contextualised? Finally, it has argued that in exploring these twin themes further, a focus on children as social actors allows us to see their participative role in the shaping of childhood itself. The final section of this chapter, therefore, is concerned with exploring the nature of children's childhoods, a theme emerging directly out of these new paradigms of child study.

That the plural 'childhoods' rather than childhood is now seen as a preferable phrasing is witness to a growing realisation within the new social studies of children that 'childhood', as much as 'adulthood', is riven and fragmented by diversity. Children are not just children; they are girls and boys, members of different social classes and diverse ethnic groups. Thus, any similarities or differences between their lives must, in part, be a function of their different membership of such groups. The previous insistence on the possibility of talking of 'the child' in abstract, rather than children in particular, simply emphasises the point that children as social actors were awarded little subjectivity in earlier discussions of childhood. This diminution of children's conscious subjectivity in such accounts of childhood underscores the even earlier suggestion that children were seen as largely 'driven' by the particularity of their biological and psychological make up.

Recent sociological and anthropological studies, however, place children's subjectivity at the centre. Through detailed ethnographic research, account is given of the ways in which children themselves contribute to the shape that childhood takes in any cultural setting. If, as Qvortrup et al. (1994) argues, the structural space for childhood is a constant in society – there will always be children and adults – then it is clear that the particular character of that structural space of 'childhood' is not only determined by macroso-cial, economic and demographic processes. Children themselves, those who at any point in time inhabit that space, may also make their presence felt and contribute to shaping what childhood is.

Connolly (1995), for example, shows how a conscious racism develops through young children's experiences in British primary schools while Christensen's (1993) work explores Danish children's understanding of illness. Drawing on a study conducted among children at a British primary school in England (James, 1993, 1995), I have argued that children have to literally embody the idea of the child. This is why a concern about the shape and size of the body is often central to their cultural practices: too big a body implies a greater age and places more demands for social responsi-bility upon the child; too small a body reduces a child's social status among his or her peers to 'baby-like'. At home, however, that small child or the one who is fat or very tall may be the loved son or daughter. He or she must engage with a very different image of the child enacted through the everyday domestic relations of the family at home. In such a formulation the process of socialisation – for that is essentially what is being described – is realised in part by the children themselves 'through the strategies and styles of behav-iour which [they] adopt across and between different social environments' (James and Prout, 1996: 50). The 'childhood' which they enact is, then, quite literally one which children themselves help to socially construct through their everyday actions.

Mayall's account of children's lives at home and school, one of the few which explores children's experiences across social domains, shows this process quite clearly:

> Children's conversations strongly suggest identification with other children and with the childhoods they experienced in common. When one girl or boy introduced a theme, others acknowledged it, picked it up and ran with it . . . [T]hey discussed: power relations at home; the character of life at home from a child's point of view; the control exercised by adults over their free time; how children's daily lives were organised and controlled by teachers; and their opportunities for activities and social groupings outside the immediate control of adults.

> (Mayall, 1996: 144)

Mayall concludes:

> Undoubtedly as a social group, children saw themselves as actors
> whose position required them to negotiate with, and occasionally fight
> against, parents and school teachers.

(Mayall, 1996: 144)

## Conclusion

The new social studies of childhood have progressed a long way
from the 1970s. The early, rather naive, debates about the social
construction of childhood have developed into a wide ranging and
increasingly sophisticated discussion within sociology and social
anthropology which has yielded a number of different approaches
to the study of children and some new and innovative methodologies. These explore both the ways in which discourses of the child
and the institution of childhood are embedded within social structure and children's responses to and experiences of their categorical
status as children.

At present four distinctive, though sometimes overlapping,
approaches can be identified which have at their centre four different models of the child (James et al., 1977). The first of these works
with a model of 'the social structural child'. Researchers explore the
ways in which childhood is embedded within the social structures of
society and the implications which this has for children's daily lives
in different countries. A second model used by researchers, which
is also focused on structural issues, is that of 'the socially constructed child'; here the concern is to explore the ways in which
children are represented, positioned and understood within particular societies as 'children', rather than simply as persons. The model
of 'the tribal child' is employed by researchers who are keen to
investigate the ways in which children create and inhabit their own
separate social worlds of childhood, while those working with 'the
minority group child model', though similarly seeing children as
central subjects in research, view them as people inhabiting an
adult, rather than a child's world. Here, then, the focus is on children's engagement with adults, and not simply, children's affairs.

Thus, each of these approaches to the study of childhood entails particular ideas about children's social position; each reflects particular methodological stances and engages with specific kinds of debates about children's everyday social experiences. Yet all fall within a broadly social constructionist framework in that they raise questions about the ways in which ideas of 'the child' come to be given concrete form in the daily lives of children in different societies. In this way, then, the early assertions about 'childhood' being an invented historical category have become more subtly rendered as accounts of the ways in which the early part of the human life course is differently conceptualised, both within and between cultures. The biological base of childhood is now more readily acknowledged, but it is seen as another context of a child's life which children learn to act within, rather than as a forceful determinant of their actions. And as we learn more of children's lives it is clear that the competencies which children have are as disparate as they are similar. Biological age, for example, gives us but a few guidelines from which to explore what children actually do. The expectations of what a 10-year-old is able to achieve vary enormously between different cultures, offering us conflicting images: as child soldier, factory worker, head of household, school child and dependent offspring or, indeed, any combination of these.

Similarly, the critique of crude socialisation perspectives which rang out in the call for child-centred studies of children's social lives has developed into a sophisticated understanding of the many and complex ways in which children engage with the socialising contexts within which they live out their everyday lives. Ethnographic studies are revealing skills and competencies, as well as ineffectiveness, in children's social behaviour and demonstrating the compliance of many, but the refusal of some, to conform to the demands of the social, physical and emotional environments within which they find themselves. Through the benefits reaped from the shifts in focus on children's social and physical development which these twin perspectives embrace, it has become clear that the socially constructed character of childhood must now be taken account of in any exploration of children's lives.

# References

Alderson, P. (1993). *Children's Consent to Surgery*. Buckingham: Open University Press.

Archard, R. (1993). *Children: Rights to Childhood*. London: Routledge.

Ariès, P. (1962). *Centuries of Childhood*. London: Cape.

Bluebond-Langner, M. (1978). *The Private Worlds of Dying Children*. Princeton, NJ: Princeton University Press.

Boswell, J. (1988). *The Kindness of Strangers: The Abandonment of Children in Western Europe from Late Antiquity to the Renaissance*. Harmondsworth: Penguin.

Boyden, J. (1990). Childhood and the policy makers: a comparative perspective on the globalisation of childhood. In: *Constructing and Reconstructing Childhood*, ed. A. James and A. Prout. Basingstoke: Falmer Press.

Briggs, J. (1986). Expecting the unexpected: Canadian Inuit training for an experimental life-style. Paper delivered to the *Fourth International Conference on Hunting and Gathering Societies*, London School of Economics.

Briggs, J. (1990). Playwork as a tool in the socialisation of the Inuit child. *Arctic Medical Research*, **49**, 34–8.

Burman, E. (1994). *Deconstructing Developmental Psychology*. London: Routledge.

Christensen, P. (1993). The social construction of help among Danish children. *Sociology of Health and Illness*, **15**, 488–502.

Connolly, P. (1995). Boys will be boys? Racism, sexuality and the construction of masculine identities among infant boys. In: *Debates and Issues in Feminist Research and Pedagogy*, ed. J. Holland, M. Blair and S. Sheldon. Clevedon: Multilingual Matters in association with OU Press.

Connolly, M. and Ennew, J. (1996). Introduction: children out of place. *Childhood*, **3**, 131–47.

Davies, B. (1982). *Life in the Classroom and Playground*. London: Routledge and Kegan Paul.

De Mause (ed.). (1976). *The History of Childhood*. London: Souvenir.

Dunn, J. (1986). Growing up in a family world: issues in the study of social development in young children. In: *Children of Social Worlds*, ed. M. Richards and P. Light. Cambridge: Polity Press.

Ennew, J. (1986). *The Sexual Exploitation of Children*. Cambridge: Polity Press.

Field, N. (1995). The child as laborer and consumer: the disappearance of childhood in contemporary Japan. In: *Children and the Politics of Culture*, ed. S. Stephens. Princeton, NJ: Princeton University Press.

Fuller, P. (1979). Uncovering childhood. In: *Changing Childhood*, ed. M. Hoyles. London: Writers and Readers Cooperative.

Hardman, C. (1973). Can there be an anthropology of children? *Journal of the Anthropology Society of Oxford*, **4**, 85–99.

Hendry, J. (1986). *Becoming Japanese.* Manchester: Manchester University Press.

Hockey, J. and James, A. (1993). *Growing Up and Growing Old.* London: Sage.

Holt, J. (1975). *Escape from Childhood.* Harmondsworth: Penguin.

Howell, S. (1987). From child to human: Chewong concepts of self. In: *Acquiring Culture*, ed. G. Jahoda and I. M. Lewis. London: Croom Helm.

James, A. (1979). Confections, concoctions and conceptions. *Journal of the Anthropology Society of Oxford*, **10**, 83–95.

James, A. (1993). *Childhood Identities: Self and Social Relationships in the Experience of the Child.* Edinburgh: Edinburgh University Press.

James, A. (1995). On being a child: the self, the group and the category. In: *Questions of Consciousness*, ed. A. P. Cohen and N. Rapport. London: Routledge.

James, A. and Jenks, C. (1996). Public perceptions of childhood criminality. *British Journal of Sociology*, **47**, 315–31.

James, A. and Prout, A. (eds). (1990). *Constructing and Reconstructing Childhood.* Basingstoke: Falmer Press.

James, A. and Prout, A. (1996). Strategies and structures: towards a new perspective on children's experiences of family life. In: *Children and Families: Research and Policy*, ed. J. Brannen and M. O'Brien. London: Falmer Press.

James, A., Jenks, C. and Prout, A. (1997). *Theorising Childhood.* Cambridge: Polity Press (in press).

Jenks, C. (ed.). (1982). *The Sociology of Childhood – Essential Readings.* London: Batsford.

Jenks, C. (1996a). The postmodern child. In: *Children and Families: Research and Policy*, ed. J. Brannen and M. O'Brien. London: Falmer Press.

Jenks, C. (1996b). *Childhood.* London: Routledge.

Johnson, V., Hill, J. and Ivan-Smith, E. (1995). *Listening to the Smaller Voices: Children in an Environment of Change.* London: Action Aid.

Light, P. (1986). Context, conservation and conversation. In: *Children of Social Worlds*, ed. M. Richards and P. Light. Cambridge: Polity Press.

Mayall, B. (1996). *Children, Health and the Social Order.* Buckingham: Open University Press.

Mead, M. and Wolfenstein, M. (eds). (1955). *Childhood in Contemporary Cultures.* Chicago: Chicago University Press.

Nieuwenhuys, O. (1994). *Children's Life Worlds: Gender, Welfare and Labour in the Developing World.* London: Routledge.

Opie, I. and Opie, P. (1959). *The Lore and Language of Schoolchildren.* Oxford: Oxford University Press.

Opie, I. and Opie, P. (1969). *Children's Games in Street and Playground.* Oxford: Oxford University Press.

Pollard, A. (1985). *The Social World of the Primary School.* London: Holt, Rhinehart and Winston.

Pollard, A. and Filer, A. (1996). *The Social World of Children's Learning*. London: Cassell.

Pollock, L. (1983). *Forgotten Children: Parent–Child Relations 1500–1900*. Cambridge: Cambridge University Press.

Postman, N. (1982). *The Disappearance of Childhood*. New York: Delacotte Press.

Prout, A. and James, A. (1990). A new paradigm for the sociology of childhood? Provenance promise and problems. In: *Constructing and Reconstructing Childhood*, ed. A. James and A. Prout. Basingstoke: Falmer Press.

Qvortrup, J., Bardy, M., Sgritta, G. and Wintersberger, H. (eds). (1994). *Childhood Matters: Social Theory, Practice and Politics*. Aldershot: Avebury.

Reynolds, P. (1996). *Traditional Healers and Childhood in Zimbabwe*. Athens: Ohio Press.

Richards, M. and Light, P. (eds). (1986). *Children of Social Worlds*. Cambridge: Polity Press.

Save the Children. (1995). *Towards a Children's Agenda*. London: Save the Children.

Shahar, S. (1990). *Childhood in the Middle Ages*. London: Routledge.

Stainton-Rogers, R. (1989). The social construction of childhood. In: *Child Abuse and Neglect*, ed. W. Stainton-Rogers, D. Harvey and E. Ash. London: Open University Press.

Stephens, S. (ed.). (1995). *Children and the Politics of Culture*. Princeton, NJ: Princeton University Press.

Thorne, B. (1993). *Gender Play*. New Jersey: Rutgers University Press.

Walkerdine, V. (1988). *The Mastery of Reason: Cognitive Development and the Production of Rationality*. London: Routledge.

Wilson, A. (1980). The infancy of the history of childhood: an appraisal of Philippe Ariès. *History and Theory*, **19**, 132–53.

Woodhead, M. (1990). Psychology and the cultural construction of children's needs. In: *Constructing and Reconstructing Childhood*, ed. A. James and A. Prout. Basingstoke: Falmer Press.

Woodhead, M. (1996). *In Search of the Rainbow: Pathways to Quality in Large-scale Programmes for Young Disadvantaged Children*. The Hague: Bernard van Leer Foundation.

# 4

## Biological anthropology and child health: context, process and outcome

CATHERINE PANTER-BRICK

## Introduction

This chapter outlines bio-anthropological contributions to the study of child health. Biological anthropologists advocate a research perspective that examines human behaviour (of men, women and children) elicited in response to external challenges from physical or socioeconomic environments. Such research seeks to document the relative costs and benefits of observed behaviours in terms of short-term and long-term consequences, particularly for health. This adaptive paradigm has been outlined elsewhere (Harrison et al., 1988; Waterlow, 1988; Carey, 1990; Ulijaszek and Strickland, 1993), but here I tie it specifically to children.

First, let us clarify why attention should be focused on children, and define the age range usually considered. Children, along with pregnant and lactating women, are commonly viewed as vulnerable groups among human communities, 'at risk' from poor environments (Prentice and Prentice, 1988). The 'at risk' groups of children have commonly been divided into infants, 0–1 year of age, and young children, 1–5 years of age. Within the field of biological anthropology, much research has focused on mother–child interactions and on children under 5 years of age, who are most dependent upon parents and other adults. In academic circles, relatively little attention, however, has been paid to the health and behaviours of 5- to 15-year-olds, except by workers linked to non-governmental organisations such as the United Nation's Children's Fund (UNICEF). UNICEF defines 'childhood' as 0–15 years of age, and its annual reports identifying health issues of special concern focus particularly on 'children in difficult circumstances' (Black, 1993; Ekberg and Mjaavatn, 1993; UNICEF, 1996).

In this chapter, I draw from studies of early (0–5 years) and late (5–15 years) childhood to illustrate cross-cultural, bio-anthropological contributions to the study of child health.

## Measuring outcomes of ill-health

For the tools of their trade, biological anthropologists have developed a number of trusted indicators of child health and ill-health. Two of the most important indicators are demographic and anthropometric parameters (Table 4.1). Because the literature on health issues is so extensive (Hansluwka, 1985), I wish here only to highlight useful means of presenting relevant data and some of the controversies regarding their interpretation.

It is worth spelling out the reasons why both demographic and anthropometric indicators have been widely used in cross-cultural studies of child health. First of all, these kinds of data are relatively

Table 4.1. *Indicators of child health: integrating measures on the outcomes of ill-health with information on social and ecological contexts*

| Macro-level data on outcomes | Contextual data |
| --- | --- |
| *Demographic indicators* | |
| Fertility | Weaning, childcare practices |
| Mortality | Birth intervals |
| Morbidity | Poverty, education |
| *Anthropometric indicators* | |
| Weight, height | Malnutrition |
| Height-for-age (stunting) | Infection |
| Weight-for-height (wasting) | Household composition |
| Weight-for-age (underweight) | |

easy to obtain – namely, information on births, deaths, heights and weights. Second, there exists a large comparative body of data for Western and non-Western populations (derived from censuses, world fertility surveys, national and community-based growth studies) available for comparative purposes. Third, both mortality and growth rates among children are considered to be sensitive to poor environmental conditions (Harrison et al., 1990; Mascie-Taylor, 1991). Thus, in developing countries like The Gambia, the 'growth rate is very clearly related to climatic factors associated with the timing of the rainy season or seasons, through their influence on food availability, parasite load . . . and infection' (Cole, 1993: 89). Childhood mortality rates have also been shown to vary seasonally in many developing countries, for example in Nepal and The Gambia (Nabarro, 1984; Ulijaszek, 1993).

## Demographic indicators

Demographers have subdivided childhood into different time intervals to better examine the rates and causes of child deaths. Thus, infant mortality refers to the number of deaths under 1 year of age (per 1000 live births), while child mortality is usually taken as the number of deaths from age 1 year to 5 years. Low infant and child mortality rates are sensitive measures of community well-being, and thus of the adequacy of public health (Allen and Thomas, 1992; Tilford, 1995; UNICEF, 1996).

In Western countries, the greatest improvements in mortality have taken place for postneonatal infant mortality through public health measures and medical care. The causes of postneonatal mortality (1–12 months of age) are mostly infections and accidents, whereas neonatal mortality (in the first month of life) is due to birth injuries, prematurity or malformations. An example will illustrate the dramatic decrease in infant deaths. In 1662, John Gaunt recorded an infant mortality in Great Britain of the order of 300 deaths per 1000 live births; by 1901, this rate was only 151 deaths, and by 1985, only 9.4 deaths per 1000 live births (Pollard et al., 1974; 68).

Developing countries can be ranked according to their infant and child mortality rates in order to draw attention to problems of poverty and ill-health. Using data from the 1976 World Fertility Survey, Hobcraft et al. (1984) showed that Senegal, Nepal and Bangladesh had the highest overall mortality rates for under-fives among 28 Third World countries (Table 4.2). Nepal and Bangladesh had the highest infant mortality (accounting for two-thirds of total deaths), while Senegal had the highest child mortality (half the deaths occurred at ages 1 to 5 years). This picture helped to pinpoint periods of childhood vulnerability, associated with extreme poverty in all three countries, and specifically in Senegal with the weaning period, after the first year of life.

Hobcraft et al. (1983) also used the World Fertility Survey to show that closely spaced births have a negative impact on mortality rates, of both the index child and subsequent children. Where birth intervals were short (less than 2 years apart), the index child showed a greater risk of mortality in nine of the 23 countries studied; this could be explained by premature weaning if the mother was newly pregnant. The subsequent child also showed an elevated risk of death (by 50%) in 13 of the countries surveyed. Two hypotheses are commonly offered to explain why short birth intervals elevate the mortality of subsequent children: a maternal depletion syndrome (whereby a mother may start her reproductive life underweight, sustains repeated pregnancies and lactation, and gives birth to a small baby,

Table 4.2. *Use of demographic indicators. National mortality rates for children in the first 5 years of life*

|  | Infant 0–1 year /1000 (%) | Child 1–5 years /1000 (%) | Under-fives 0–5 years /1000 (%) |
|---|---|---|---|
| Senegal | 123[6] (43) | 164[1] (57) | 287[1] (100) |
| Nepal | 166[1] (64) | 93[2] (36) | 259[2] (100) |
| Bangladesh | 141[2] (66) | 74[3] (34) | 215[3] (100) |

*Notes:*
Superscripts are rankings among 28 Third World countries.
*Source:* Data from Hobcraft et al. (1984). World Fertility Survey (1976).

which has poorer chances of survival), and sibling competition (for scarce household resources or maternal attention). Thus, demographers have shown that birth interval, along with mother's education (Cleland and van Ginneken, 1988), emerges as one of the most significant factors to influence variation in mortality rates for children under 5 years of age (Hobcraft et al., 1985).

Anthropologists have also used these indicators to characterise the health consequences of childcare behaviours at community or household level. For instance, Hewlett (1991) reviewed the extent to which demographic parameters (total fertility, infant and child mortality, age and sex composition) explained cross-cultural variation in childcare practices (such as single versus multiple caregiving, male-biased sex ratios and step-parenting) among hunter/gatherers, horticulturalists and pastoralists. This type of analysis provides a useful socioecological context to data on mortality rates, which are otherwise used at a global level as indicators of community health (Newell and Nabarro, 1989) (Table 4.1).

## Anthropometric indicators

Slow growth is also an excellent indicator of poor environmental conditions affecting past, present and future health (Mascie-Taylor, 1991). A very large number of growth studies have focused on the first few years of life when children should experience rapid physical development but are very vulnerable to growth retardation (Tanner and Preece, 1989). I will here illustrate useful representations of growth data with two examples from anthropological field studies.

Failure to thrive from birth until 24 months of age is illustrated in Figure 4.1 for Turkana pastoralist children in Kenya. Here the growth status of children is shown in terms of absolute weights and lengths, plotted against percentiles of the US reference population (while other reference populations are available (Cole, 1990), the US data set from the National Center for Health Statistics (NCHS) (Hamill et al., 1979) have been recommended by the World Health Organization (1986)). Up to 9 months, the average weight of Turk-

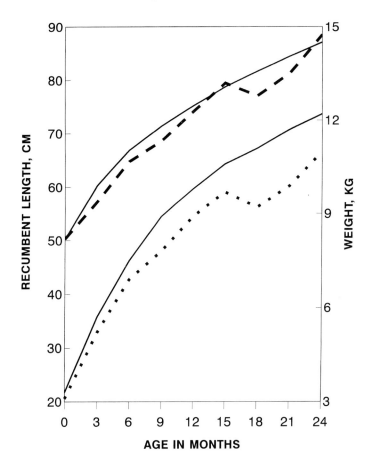

Figure 4.1. Growth of Turkana 0- to 24-month-old infants, plotted against the 50th percentile of the US reference data from the National Center of Health Statistics. After Gray (1998).

ana children is just below the 50th percentile but after that age there is a gradual deceleration of weight gain. In the Turkana community, therefore, children are vulnerable to growth retardation after age 9 months. They recover growth velocity only after age 2 years (Gray, 1998).

Growth retardation can be illustrated in another way by plotting heights and weights as standard deviations from the reference population. In Figure 4.2, growth status is indicated by the extent of deviation (z-scores) from the median of the US reference

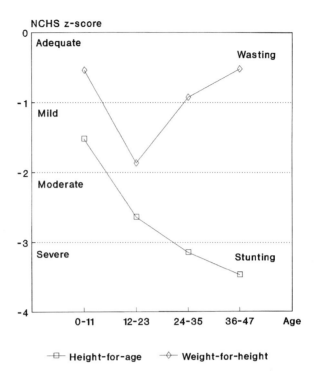

Figure 4.2. Thresholds of growth retardation, relative to standard deviations (z-scores) from the National Center of Health Statistics reference population, and measures for 70 Nepali 0–48 months old rural children, in the rainy season. After Panter-Brick (1997).

population. A child with a z-score of zero is identical in height-for-age or weight-for-height to an average child in the USA of the same age and sex. Increasing growth retardation is indicated by increasingly large negative z-scores. The recommended cut-off points defining growth retardation are −2 standard deviations (SD) for stunting (height-for-age, HAz), wasting (weight-for-height, WHz), or underweight (weight-for-age, WAz). Z-scores also help to classify the proportion of children with adequate (+1 to −1 SD), mild (−1 to −2 SD), moderate (−2 to −3 SD) or severe (below −3 SD) anthropometric status (Hamill et al., 1979). These scores can be conveniently calculated from assembled data sets using simple computer packages (e.g. EPI-INFO and EPI-NUT) (Dean et al.,

1990). As seasonality, however, imposes periodic stresses on children's rates of growth in many parts of the world, such estimates of growth retardation, which rely on absolute cut-off points, may well differ from season to season.

Figure 4.2 shows the growth status for 0- to 4-year-old children, both sexes combined, in a remote rural area of Nepal (Panter-Brick, 1997). Their growth pattern is characterised by moderate to severe stunting (the overall NCHS z-score for height-for-age (mean −2.61, SD 1.22) is between −2 and −3), but not extensive wasting (the z-score for weight-for-height (mean −0.91, SD 0.91) is not below −1 SD; Panter-Brick, 1997). Thus, the children grow up to be very small in height, but stocky. Very much the same picture is noted in The Gambia. In both rural (Rowland et al., 1981) and urban (Tomkins et al., 1986a,b) areas, there is prevalent stunting but no wasting for Gambian children, even at the height of the rainy season. While height-for-age worsened from 6 to 35 months of age, low weight-for-height affected only 9% of children (Tomkins et al., 1986b: 110).

Typically in Third World populations, growth starts to falter at 3 months of age and is significant by 18 months (United Nations, 1993; Martorell et al., 1994). Wasting occurs at 1 and 2 years of age when children are given supplementary foods and thereby exposed to infections. Stunting worsens after age 1 year, when children fall further behind international reference values. Thus, at 12 months of age, the rural Nepali children average 69 cm and 7 kg (Panter-Brick, 1997), rural Gambian children average 70 cm and 8 kg (Cole, 1993: 97), whereas children in the USA average 75 cm and 10 kg (NCHS reference data). At 24 months of age, the Nepali children are 77 cm and just under 9 kg, the Gambian children 80 cm and not quite 10 kg, while children in the USA have reached 86 cm and 12 kg.

These patterns of growth have consequences in later childhood, and of course for final adult height. Figure 4.3 presents the profiles of four groups of Nepali 6- to 14-year-olds, who still show moderate stunting but no wasting. The impact of rural–urban and socioeconomic differences on growth status is also illustrated in this figure: poor village children, who eat a bulky, monotonous diet low in fat and pro-

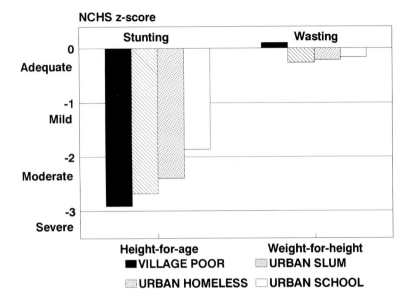

Figure 4.3. Growth status of 6- to 14-year-old boys in Nepal showing rural–urban and socioeconomic differentials in a remote village, Kathmandu slums, streets and middle-class school (girls show the same profile). After Panter-Brick et al. (1996a).

tein, engage in daily work and sustain chronic infections, achieve smaller stature than urban counterparts, even compared with those homeless on the streets (Panter-Brick et al., 1996a). These differentials are well documented for other populations in Peru, Papua New Guinea and The Gambia (Leonard, 1989; Cole, 1993; Zemel et al., 1993). It is not easy, however, to pinpoint the relative influence of multiple environmental, genetic and maturational factors responsible for the observed anthropometric variation.

How significant are these differences in growth patterns? The consequences of short stature, for instance, were the subject of much debate in the 1980s. It was suggested that being small but stocky, or 'small but healthy', was an appropriate response to poor socioeconomic conditions because it takes less food to sustain a smaller body size when food supplies are limited (Seckler, 1982). This view has been forcefully rejected as one that ignores evidence for the real costs associated with smallness (reduced work capacity, activity and reproductive success (Martorell, 1989) and, moreover, justifies the social and political indifference to the plight of the world's poor (Gopalam, 1983). Growth retardation as a response to poor environmental conditions is best regarded not as an adaptation but as an accommodation – adaptation describes a beneficial response to poor environments, while the term accommodation draws attention to both the costs and benefits of a coping behaviour (Scrimshaw and Young, 1989; Frisancho, 1993).

One criticism levelled at many growth studies has been over-reliance on anthropometric measures: the sine qua non of nutrition policy and intervention. For example, in famine situations low height-for-age and thin mid-arm circumference have been used to identify which children are most at risk of death and malnutrition. Growth monitoring has been promoted as a key element of primary health care and interventions, such as 'Child Survival and Development' led by UNICEF (Nabarro and Chinnock, 1988). As Beaton (1989: 32) emphasised, we fell 'into a trap of assuming that anthropometry is an adequate proxy for nutrition rather than an index of one aspect of nutritional status . . . With the proliferation of growth studies, small size changed from *being a predictor* of an undesirable health outcome to *being* the undesirable outcome' (italics in original). Despite extensive research on a range of health indicators (Hansluwka, 1985) and models showing the complexity of childhood health, and in particular the importance of infection (Mosley and Chen, 1984), a simplistic equation is often made between slow growth and poor nutrition.

A cross-sectional view of growth status offers little information regarding the processes by which children fail to thrive. Figure 4.4 illustrates this point. Here a cross-sectional survey is carried out to identify thin children, typically in a school setting (where data collection is facilitated on a captive audience), in order to determine the prevalence of childhood malnutrition from the usual cut-off points of height and weight for age. The identification of thin children, however, can tell us little about the factors associated with malnutrition: they indicate how many children are underweight but not why. In contrast, a focus on family relationships within the household can help determine the causes of malnutrition, helping to illustrate a number of different possible scenarios responsible for malnutrition. Thus, a child is thin because:

a.  He/she is one of six children (an appropriate intervention might therefore be family planning).
b.  He/she is one of two children (one should investigate possible sex differences in food allocation or access to health care).
c.  He/she has a mother but no father (this relates to problems of absolute poverty in female-headed households).

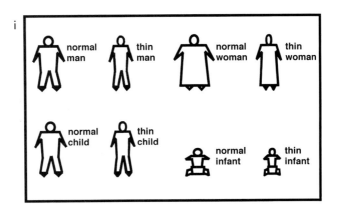

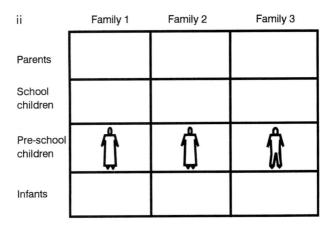

Figure 4.4. Importance of household composition for contextualising cross-sectional measures of growth status. (i) Legend. (ii) Cross-sectional survey identifying thin children. Drawings are by courtesy of Dr Dugdale.

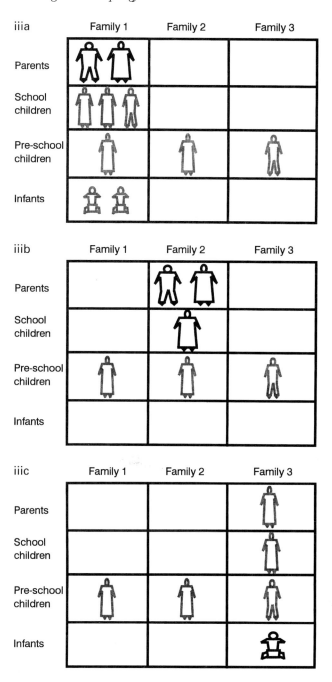

Fig. 4.4. *cont.* (iii) Scenarios of households with: (a) six children, (b) a male and female child, (c) only one parent,

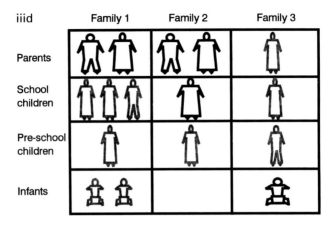

Fig. 4.4. *cont.* (d) growth status seen in the context of household composition.

These scenarios illustrate how important it is to contextualise growth retardation, with the example here of household composition. Anthropologists have cautioned against over-reliance on large-scale cross-sectional surveys of children at the expense of detailed studies of household relationships. The quality of childcare is surely different among single-parent families (such as female-headed households where fathers are absent for long periods of time) versus extended households (where two or three adult women may help in child supervision). Complex interactions between income and household head have also been documented (Kennedy and Peters, 1992). The nature of women's work and childcare arrangements, and their impact on child health, deserve particularly detailed attention (Panter-Brick, 1992). Given long-term familiarity with local communities, resulting from extensive periods of fieldwork, anthropologists are best at offering in-depth and multi-disciplinary information on social and ecological settings in order to shed light on the processes of growth retardation. As Beaton (1989: 37) emphasised, 'it is not *being* small that matters. Rather it is *becoming* small that is critically important' (italics in original). Hence, 'we must focus on the process of becoming small and on the environmental factors – biological and social – that are the determinants of smallness'.

Other studies have examined growth variability as an index of environmental quality. Growth faltering or catch-up growth reflect changes in an individual's fitness in favourable or adverse environments (Harrison, 1993). Here attention is focused on the variance of growth increments rather than the size of the increments, namely acceleration rather than mere distance (Harrison et al., 1990). Frequent (e.g. weekly or daily) measurements of variance help to document the nature of growth processes (which may be episodic, rather than linear) (Lampl, 1993; Lampl and Johnson, 1997) and disaggregate the genetic and environmental components of character variability (Harrison, 1993; Johnston 1995). Thus, growth velocity can provide further contextual information on the impact of various constraints affecting childhood health. Overall, then, as Tanner (1986) explicitly articulated, the growth of children can be held as 'a mirror of the condition of society'.

## Measuring the processes of ill-health

Indicators of mortality and growth status per se are useful but serve to measure the outcome (death, malnutrition) rather than the process (adaptability, vulnerability, resilience) by which children cope with difficult environments (Table 4.3). Let us now focus on indicators which are useful for examining the *processes* by which children become unhealthy (as opposed to the final *outcomes*, counting dead and thin children).

### Infection and malnutrition

There is a very large body of literature on childhood infection and malnutrition, swelling evidence of early studies on the synergistic relations between these two variables (Mosley and Chen, 1984). The approaches to evaluating the importance of infections have included clinical trials (measuring growth outcome for infected children and controls, having determined infection load) and naturalistic field studies (identifying significant predictors of poor growth status or growth velocity, by multiple regression analyses, from

Table 4.3. *Indicators of child health: examining the processes contributing to ill-health*

| Coping processes | Assessment |
| --- | --- |
| Adaptability<br>Vulnerability<br>Resilience | Infection load<br>Immunocompetence |
| | Food intake<br>Food distribution |
| | Physical activity<br>Work patterns |
| | Psychosocial well-being<br>Stress reactivity |

detailed data on morbidity). A rather different approach recently attempted by anthropologists is to relate immune function (immunocompetence) to patterns of growth and morbidity for populations in given local environments.

For instance, Shell-Duncan (1993) tested the immunocompetence of 64 nomadic Turkana children, 6 months to 10 years of age. She injected subcutaneously five specific antigens, plus a non-reactive control, and measured the induration (skin reaction produced by T lymphocytes) produced 48 hours later – this is called delayed-type hypersensitivity (DTH) testing. Over half the children tested showed significant suppression of their immune system (induration <2 mm). Turkana children suffered 1.65 and 1.38 episodes of acute respiratory infection and 0.64 and 1.41 episodes of gastrointestinal infection per month of surveillance in the wet and dry seasons, respectively (Shell-Duncan and Wood, 1997). Year-round susceptibility to infection, rather than poor dietary intake, explained their chronic mild-to-moderate growth retardation and the lack of seasonal variation in growth mesurements. Suppressed immunity was a significant predictor of morbidity, leading to an excess of acute respiratory (34%) and diarrhoeal (20%) attacks relative to immunocompetent children.

Given that gastrointestinal and acute respiratory infections are the two leading causes of deaths in the Third World (WHO, 1992), the suggestion that immune function mediates the relation between malnutrition and infection is clearly important (Shell-Duncan and Wood, 1997). In Peru and Bangladesh also, downregulation of immune function has been implicated in childhood morbidity from persistent diarrhoea, while malnutrition as an independent risk factor has been variously implicated (Koster et al., 1987; Black et al., 1989; Baqui et al., 1993, Shell-Duncan, 1997). Greater attention to incidence, severity, duration and type of diseases, as well as seasonal and age covariates, will further unravel the complex links between nutritional status, growth velocity and infectious morbidity (Panter-Brick, 1997).

Research on patterns of food intake accounting for poor nutrition has been fraught with difficulties of measurement and observation (Huss-Ashmore, 1996). For example, young children often breast-feed up to 3 years of age, eat solid food from a communal dish and snack away from home. None the less, some careful studies have managed to document intrahousehold food allocation leading to the positive or negative treatment of children relative to their age, economic contribution or prospects of survival (Pelto, 1984; Leonard and Thomas, 1989; Scheper-Hughes, 1991; Dettwyler, 1992). One anthropological study has provided valuable information on the social context of intrahousehold food distribution, observing family behaviour at meal times and recording priority in serving order, refusals or requests for extra helpings, as well as quality and quantity of food items (Gittelsohn, 1991). The study emphasised not just *who* receives preferential treatment, but *how* biases in food distribution are actually shown. Thus, in Nepal, children received top priority in serving order and high quality food, yet their intakes were insufficient as they rarely received second helpings at meal time.

## *Physical activity*

Another sphere of concern is to measure children's levels of physical activity. Methods of assessment include use of doubly labelled water (expensive), measurements of energy expenditure by indirect calorimetry (cumbersome) and monitoring of heart rate (an estimate of activity). Yet despite the availability of research methods, relatively few cross-cultural studies of children's physical activity levels have been made to date. I here review heart rate monitoring because it seems particularly well suited to cross-cultural comparisons of children in free-living situations, especially for the older group of 5- to 15-year-olds. It also yields good quality data while being non-invasive and is generally perceived as 'good fun' from the point of view of the children themselves.

Studies in Western countries have recently expressed concern regarding children's habitually low levels of physical activity. The lifestyle of pre-adolescent children (dubbed 'TV couch potatoes' or 'young slobs') (Saul, 1994; Malina, 1995) is deemed to involve insufficient levels of high intensity exercise, which is thought to promote cardiovascular fitness and confer protection against the risks of coronary heart disease, diabetes and oesteoporosis in adulthood. Indeed, the Broadcasting Audience Research Board showed that 'in 1993, British 4–15 year olds watch an average 2–3 hours of television a day', while 'The National Curriculum for schools allocates an average of only 1 hour a week for physical education, and in practise less than 10% of this time is spent exercising' (Saul, 1994: 24). A study by Armstrong et al. (1990) found that British 11- to 16-year-olds spent only 6% of a 12-hour day (43 minutes) at heart rates above 139 beats per minute, roughly 70% of the maximal heart rate (Table 4.4). A third of children were not active enough to raise their heart rates to the equivalent of a brisk 10-minute walk a day (quoted in Saul, 1994). One literature review found that 6- to 13-year-olds (mostly Western children) spent 15–40 minutes/day in moderate and 4–22 minutes/day in high intensity activities (where $HR = 150–169$ and $HR > 169$ beats per minute, respectively (Riddoch and Boreham, 1995)). The relations between physical exercise, cardiovascular fitness and disease, however, are debated for adults and even more so for children (Malina, 1995; Riddoch and Boreham, 1995). The assumption that increased vigorous physical activity in childhood translates into long-term benefits to cardiovascular health is 'intuitively attractive, but largely untested' (Livingstone et al., 1992: 351).

Surprisingly, a cluster of studies in the developing world, where

Table 4.4. *Indicators of physical activity among children:[a] mean day-time heart rates and percentage time in vigorous activity (above 139 beats per minute)*

| | Age (years) | Observed time (hours) | n boys | Day-time heart rate Mean (SD) | Vigorous activity % time (SD) |
|---|---|---|---|---|---|
| British school[b] | 11–16 | 12 | 103 | NA | 6.2 NA |
| Irish school[c] | 12–15 | <16 | 8 | NA | 3.1 (1.9) |
| | 12 | | 5 | 104 | 3.2 (2.2) |
| | 15 | | 3 | 97 | 2.2 (1.4) |
| Senegal farmers[d] | 11–16 | NA | 37 | NA | 1.7 (0.7) |
| | 12–13 | | NA | 99 (2) | NA |
| | 14–15 | | NA | 93 (13) | NA |
| Senegal farmers[e] | 10–12 | 6 | 17 | NA | 4.1 (4.2) |
| | 12–14 | 6 | 28 | NA | 2.6 (3.0) |
| Nepal (4 groups)[f] | 10–13 | 10 | 67 | 102 (10) | 4 (5) |

*Notes:*
[a] Only data on boys are shown here.
[b] Armstrong et al. (1990). HR >139 bpm, roughly 70% of the maximal HR.
[c] Livingstone et al. (1992). HR >50% of peak oxygen uptake for 'moderate vigorous physical activity', corresponding to HR >147 bpm.
[d] Diaham and Prentice (1993). HR >140 bpm for 'intense' activity.
[e] Bénéfice (1992). HR >140 bpm.
[f] Panter-Brick et al. (1996b). HR >139 bpm for 'vigorous activity' among village, urban slum, homeless street and middle-class school children.

one would presume children to be far more physically active, conclude that the lifestyle of rural children involves even fewer periods of vigorous physical activity (Table 4.4). In Senegal, 10- to 16-year-olds in a rural subsistence community spent only 2–4% of their day at heart rate elevations above 139 beats per minute (Bénéfice, 1992; Diaham and Prentice, 1993). In Nepal also, 10- to 13-year-olds spent 4% of their day above this threshold (Panter-Brick et al., 1996b). These low levels of vigorous physical activity probably reflect a tendency to spend relatively more time working at a moderate rather than a vigorous pace, in order to avoid physical exhaustion and to be able to sustain agricultural activities throughout the working day. Rural Nepali boys, for example, were active for 73% (at rest for only 27%) of daylight hours, moderately active for 33% and vigorously active for just 5% of the day (as measured by increasing thresholds of heart rate elevations). An absolute cut-off point of heart rate elevation (e.g. 139 beats per minute to define exertion), however, does not take into account possible differences in physical fitness across populations resulting from habitual levels of physical activity.

Simple indicators of heart rate elevation do not adequately differentiate levels of physical activity. This is true for mean day-time heart rates in particular. While 12-year-old Irish boys averaged 104 beats per minute over one weekend and two school days, Senegalese 12-year-olds working on farms averaged only 99 beats per minute over the observation day (Table 4.4). Four groups of Nepali boys (rural children, urban slum-dwelling, homeless and middle-class school children) all averaged 102 beats per minute, despite their contrasting lifestyles. Mean day-time heart rates equally failed to discriminate between groups of mildly malnourished and adequately nourished schoolboys in Colombia (100 and 99 beats per minute) (Spurr et al., 1986), even though the former could not keep up with better nourished counterparts during organised strenuous sport (Spurr and Reina, 1988). The use of heart rate threshold values to grade the intensity of physical activity is a valuable approach, but unfortunately different studies have used discrepant cut-off points to define moderate and vigorous physical activity (Riddoch and Boreham, 1995). Rather than a day-time average, or absolute thresholds of heart rate elevation, indicators of physical activity should rely on heart rate values calibrated for individual children. It is appropriate, for instance, to use percentage times spent in excess of individually calibrated rest and exercise heart rates (Panter-Brick et al., 1996b), or percentage times of the heart rate measured at maximal oxygen consumption (Spurr and Reina, 1990), as is done when energy expenditures are inferred from heart rates (Spurr et al., 1986).

Studies of physical activity levels also need to include detailed quantitative observations of habitual behaviour. In the field of child health, documentation of what 5- to 15-year-olds actually do in rural or urban communities of the developing world has rarely gone beyond the presentation of macrolevel data on child wage labour and school enrolment, or of reported data on children's daily time allocation from interviews with small samples of caregivers. We know that many children are employed in the domestic economy and some in wage labour at a very young age (Fyfe, 1985; Weiner, 1991), but there has been little quantification of actual workloads coupled with a thorough exploration of health correlates, despite widespread anthropological interest and humanitarian concern with child labour. Some early studies interested in the economic value of children have gathered data on time-inputs in domestic and subsistence activities. Thus, Cain (1977), who collected information on household time-budgets by interview, concluded that Bangladeshi children began useful productive tasks at age 6 years, worked as long or longer (9 hours a day) than adults by age 13 years and, if male, were already net economic producers in their household when 12 years old. Similarly, Nag et al. (1978) gathered data (by interview) for 6- to 19-year-olds in rural Java and Nepal. In percentage terms, 7-year-olds completed close to a third, 10-year-olds a half and 13-year-olds three-quarters of the work of adults. Girls did more than boys, and were involved in handicrafts and childcare, while boys spent up to 5 hours a day involved in animal care. In turn Nieuwenhuys (1994), who combined interviews with observations on children themselves, showed how early work responsibilities constrained gender opportunities to participate in school and other social networks in Kerala, India. Both boys and girls aged 5–15 years spent a total 7 hours a day working in domestic, waged and unwaged work, but girls were co-opted more often to work in housekeeping and childcare which increasingly bound them to the home environment.

Another study, this time based on systematic, quantitative spot-check observations, showed that by 6 or 7 years, rural Kipsigis in Kenya spent more time working on household chores than they did resting or playing (Super and Harkness, 1986). It was concluded: 'in contrast to the middle-class Western emphasis on play as central to young children's development, work was clearly the main task of childhood' for the Kipsigis (p. 554).

In farming communities, children's work is expedient for parents who experience chronic or acute shortages of manpower (Figure 4.5). Thus, Thomas (1976) and Leonard and Thomas (1989) concluded that child labour among the Andean Quechua was an adaptive strategy at the household level, as tasks such as herding were less energetically expensive for children to complete than for adults. The extent of a child's participation in the household economy may even be detected in growth status (Stinson, 1980).

By contrast to children in agricultural contexts, hunter–gatherer !Kung children 'do amazingly little work', as Draper (1976: 213) showed with a time allocation study based on spot-check observations. A more experimental approach to develop an understanding of children's behaviour was taken by Blurton Jones et al. (1994): they scheduled 'experimental' foraging excursions in two hunter–gatherer communities to evaluate the costs and benefits of children's foraging work. This helped to show why !Kung children seldom help adults forage for food in contrast to the Hadza who, at 7 years of age, routinely walk a 10 km round trip to berry groves.

Another example of studies offering quantitative data on young people's activities is that of Malville and Malville (1996). They interviewed a total of 339 hill porters in Nepal, on a trail of 95 km and 1500 m elevation, and measured the heart rate profile of volunteers during load-carrying. Most had started commercial portering at age 15 years, when rural Nepali youths join the adult work force, but many had begun at a younger age. The young porters, 11–15 years of age, carried loads of 48 kg (106 lb), equivalent to 134% of their body weight. Half of them were students working during school holidays.

Besides subsistence and waged labour, children also care for their siblings (Figure 4.6). Social anthropologist Weisner (1982) was among the first to focus attention on children's roles in sib–sib care. Yet this role for children is largely seen by biomedical practitioners in a negative light. In The Gambia, adolescent girls who cared for infants while their mothers worked in the fields have been called

Figure 4.5. Twelve-year-old boy carrying a load of maize weighing 33 kg or 130% of his own body weight. Photograph by C. Panter-Brick.

Figure 4.6. Ten-year-old girl carrying one of her sisters in rural Nepal.
Photograph by C. Panter-Brick.

'incompetent nursemaids' (Lawrence et al., 1985), as poorly prepared or leftover foods, contaminated by bacteria, led to high morbidity and mortality. The strategy of alloparental care must also be
viewed in the light of the host of factors constraining mothers who
work outside the home (Lewis, 1993; Panter-Brick, 1995).

Other studies have been concerned with the consequences of

children's behaviours for mental as well as physical well-being. Thus, physical activity, particularly play, is curtailed in children limited by energy (Pollitt, 1995). To date the links between play behaviour, physical and mental health (Malina, 1992) are not fully charted.

## Stress and well-being

Lastly, I focus on a perspective that addresses psychosocial well-being, rather than frank ill-health: a new but fast developing area. Stress and well-being are dimensions of an individual's health that are particularly difficult to operationalise and measure – bio-anthropological studies are currently using hormonal, immunological and cardiovascular variables to evaluate the range of physiological responses to challenging situations (Dressler, 1995). I focus below on cross-cultural studies of hormonal stress, using urinary or salivary assays of cortisol.

Twenty years ago, Peck (1978), quoted by Sorensen (1993), emphasised that 'we know very well why people become . . . ill. What we don't understand is why people survive the traumas of their lives as well as they do . . . We know a great deal more about the causes of physical disease than we do about the causes of physical health' (pp. 237–9). Sorensen remarks that most studies in the 1980s have concentrated on adults and there has been little exploration of health, stress and coping responses in the daily lives of children (p. viii).

Some researchers have begun to address this issue in children; the results obtained and methods employed are exciting. Flinn and England (1997) have studied 264 children (age 2 months to 18 years) from 82 households in a rural village of the Caribbean island of Dominica over the past 8 years. They coupled hormonal data from multiple saliva samples ($n = 22\,438$ at the last count) with detailed ethnographic data on residence histories and individual personalities, behavioural observations and clinical information on symptoms of ill-health. Their objective was an in-depth study of family environments and childhood stress response. The results show that household composition, which is often changing in the

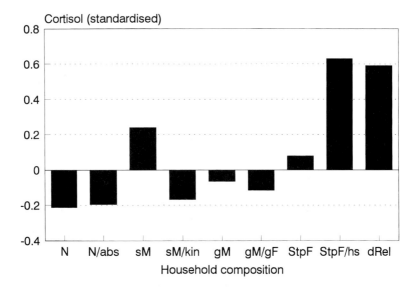

Figure 4.7. Household composition and average cortisol levels (244–6397 cortisol assays for sample sizes of 5–88 children in each household category: N: nuclear; N/abs: nuclear with father absent; sM: single mother; sM/kin: single mother + kin; gM: grandmother; gM/gF: grandparents; StpF: stepfather; StpF/hs: stepfather and half-sibs; dRel: distant relatives. From Flinn and England (1995: 858, 1997: 44).

Caribbean, has strong associations with cortisol profiles. For instance, children living with either distant relatives, stepfathers or single mothers without kin support have significantly higher cortisol profiles than children living with both parents, single parents with kin or grandparents (Figure 4.7). Here cortisol values are standardised by time of day since wake-up time, to correct for circadian variation and plotted as standard deviations from the averages of all samples taken at a given time interval. Another striking finding is that the average cortisol levels of stepchildren is significantly higher than those of biological children living in the same household (Flinn and England, 1995: 859, 1977: 43). Indeed, children in households experiencing marital conflict show abnormally higher cortisol profiles following events of discord. A parent's absence was also found to affect cortisol values, even if absences and returns are not always perceived as negative events. Cortisol

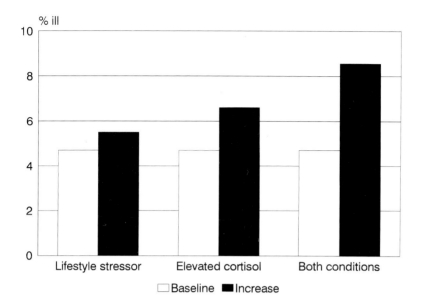

Figure 4.8. Impact of lifestyle stressor and elevated cortisol on episodes of ill-health. From M. V. Flinn (personal communication).

profiles were elevated with brief absences of the mother, especially in the case of boys, although this effect attenuated with age. While a father's temporary absence had no sequel, a prolonged absence had significant impact on boys' cortisol levels, but not on girls' (Flinn et al., 1996: 146). Thus, father's presence is especially significant for males. These associations of family composition on endocrine profiles appear to persist into adulthood. The conclusion that family composition may have an important effect on child development resonates with the situation of Western children with divorced parents who experience more stress than those living in stable nuclear families (Flinn et al., 1996: 126).

These data are very rich, particularly as episodes of ill-health seem to follow changes in cortisol response: morbidity (principally from upper respiratory tract infections) is elevated by 17% above baseline levels following a lifestyle stressor (e.g. family fight, school examinations), by 31% following a rise of cortisol levels and by 82% where both these conditions concur (Figure 4.8). Illnesses occur with a lag of 3 to 5 days, returning to baseline levels by a week's time. This study is one of a few able to relate altered hormonal profiles to incidences of ill-health.

Cortisol is often taken as a measure of anxiety, stimulated by uncertainty. It is a 'key hormone produced in response to physical and psychosocial stressors' (Flinn et al., 1996: 127). It allows the body to respond to short-term environmental challenges by regulating a wide range of physiological functions, such as the release of energy, immune activity, mental alertness, growth and reproductive function. Thus, cortisol response can be viewed as an adaptive mechanism to re-allocate energy resources in the body, in response to changing environmental conditions, with significant consequences for health in terms of physical and psychological development.

The collection of this kind of hormonal data is an attractive method for anthropological field studies because it is simple in execution and non-invasive (Baum and Grunberg, 1995). Yet the manipulation of data has to be careful and interpretation may be difficult (Pollard, 1995). First, data must be adjusted for confounding variables, such as physical activity, a rise in values after meals and the circadian fall after waking (Flinn and England, 1995). Second, different hormones may reflect distinct aspects of an individual's reactivity. For example, the study by Long et al. (1993) of 4- to 9-year-old British school children showed that cortisol and adrenaline (epinephrine), two 'stress hormones', had distinct profiles in the home and the school environments. Third, as Pollard (1995: 271) emphasised, 'cortisol does not appear to behave simply as a "stress hormone" '; it reflects general emotional arousal rather than just distress. Furthermore, low cortisol levels may indicate low external stress, or else a blunted response to stress. For instance, among Nepali 10- to 14-year-olds, cortisol values were surprisingly low among homeless, slum, school and village boys (averaging 0.18–0.27 μg/dL, by comparison to published cortisol values for children of 0.23–0.66 μg/dL; Panter-Brick et al., 1996c). While homeless boys averaged higher mean cortisol values than villagers, they showed low cortisol variance, indicating low reactivity to day-to-day events, despite the apparent insecurity of their way of life. Ethnographic data also indicated that, for many street children,

coping with homelessness entailed a blunted response to the stressful circumstances of day-to-day life.

In the light of these difficulties, research on the hormonal correlates of health and well-being will need to focus on actual variation
in hormonal levels, not only between groups of children, but also
within individuals across time and environmental settings. For
instance, changes in baseline levels may be more informative than
comparison of absolute levels of the hormone cortisol (Flinn et al.,
1996). This will necessitate more longitudinal, rather than cross-
sectional, samples with a fine-grained description of individual life
history and ecological settings.


## Conclusion

The issue of child health is of major concern and efforts have been
made to develop good indicators of child fitness, survival, health
and well-being. Thus, measures of mortality, growth status, morbidity, nutrition, physical activity and psychosocial well-being
(Tables 4.1 and 4.3) provide a 'window' on the adequacy of child
health across cultures and allow for monitoring of health care interventions. A comprehensive picture of child health is obtained by
triangulating methods and indicators, but this usually requires comparative samples, longitudinal and multi-disciplinary data.

Such indicators are very useful, although often they serve to measure the outcome (death, disease, malnutrition) rather than the process (adaptability, vulnerability, resilience) by which children cope
with difficult environments. Biological anthropologists have a long-
standing interest in the range of human coping strategies and the
limits of adaptability to poor environments. Recently, interest has
shifted from an emphasis on children's vulnerability to documenting their resilience in difficult environments (Garmezy, 1983;
Sorensen, 1993; Werner, 1993; Caldwell, 1996; Engle et al. 1996).
There has also been a resurgence of interest focusing on older
groups of children (5–15 years old) where there is much potential
for studies of 'well-being' and documentation of children's own

behavioural strategies, moving beyond a traditional outlook on 'ill-health' as measured by mortality rates and growth status.

A more thorny problem is to consider whether these indicators of health and well-being can be applied cross-culturally without a great deal of circumspection. Biomedical measures of childhood growth and mortality have been elevated to gold standards in the evaluation of health status. They have thus featured prominently in the formulation of fundamental and universal rights for children (in the 1989 Convention on the Rights of the Child) and of priorities for health intervention (in the 1990 World Summit for Children; detailed in the Glossary of this volume). Notwithstanding, there are critical differences in parental appreciation of child health and malnutrition across the West and the Third World (Cassidy, 1987; Dettwyler, 1992). For instance, mothers in dire economic conditions may selectively neglect infants who show little chance of survival (Scheper-Hughes, 1991) – here the Western biomedical emphasis on child survival alone, without alleviating household poverty, is misplaced. Also in some communities, giving plentiful or nutritious food to children is not necessarily a cultural imperative (Dettwyler, 1992). Engle and Nieves (1993) have contrasted the rules of 'need versus contribution' which determine food allocation to children: needs for growth and development versus potential contribution to the household. Again, child labour is decried in the West (Fyfe, 1985) but is seen as proper behaviour in many rural subsistence and poor urban communities (Weiner, 1991). Given that other societies may prioritise children's 'duties' rather than 'rights' or 'needs', recommendations for psychological as well as physical development should be sensitive to the existence of different cultural perspectives on childhood (Woodhead, 1990; Kağitçibaşi, 1996: 28–31; Chapters 3 and 5). In summary, it is worth appraising the range of alternative views which pertain to health and well-being, child behaviour and development, in cross-cultural contexts.

# References

Allen, T. and Thomas, A. (eds). (1992). *Poverty and Development in the 1990s.* Oxford: Oxford University Press.

Armstrong, N., Balding, J., Gentle, P. and Kirby, B. (1990). Patterns of physical activity among 11 to 16 year old British children. *British Medical Journal*, **301**, 203–5.

Baqui, A. H., Sack, R. B., Black, R. E., Chowdhury, H. R., Yunus, M. and Siddique, A. K. (1993). Cell-mediated immune deficiency and malnutrition are independent risk factors for persistent diarrhea in Bangladeshi children. *American Journal of Clinical Nutrition*, **58**, 543–8.

Baum, A. and Grunberg, N. (1995). Measurement of stress hormones. In: *Measuring Stress – A Guide for Health and Social Scientists*, ed. S. Cohen, R. C. Kessler and L. U. Gordon, pp. 175–92. Oxford: Oxford University Press.

Beaton, G. H. (1989). Small but healthy? Are we asking the right question? *Human Organization*, **48**, 30–9.

Bénéfice, E. (1992). Physical activity and anthropometric and functional characteristics of mildly nourished children. *Annals of Tropical Paediatrics*, **12**, 55–66.

Black, M. (1993). Street and Working Children. *Innocenti Global Seminar Summary Report*. Florence, Italy: UNICEF.

Black, R. E., Lanata, C. F. and Lazo, F. (1989). Delayed cutaneous hypersensitivity: epidemiologic factors affecting and usefulness in predicting diarrheal incidence in young Peruvian children. *Paediatric Infectious Diseases*, **8**, 210–15.

Blurton Jones, N., Hawkes, K. and Draper, P. (1994). Foraging patterns of !Kung adults and children: why didn't !Kung children forage? *Journal of Anthropological Research*, **50**, 217–48.

Cain, M. (1977). The economic activities of children in a village in Bangladesh. *Population and Development Review*, **3**, 201–27.

Caldwell, P. (1996). Child survival: physical vulnerability and resilience in adversity in the European past and the contemporary third world. *Social Science and Medicine*, **43**, 609–19.

Carey, J. W. (1990). Social system effects on local level morbidity and adaptation in the rural Peruvian Andes. *Medical Anthropology Quarterly*, **4**, 266–95.

Cassidy, C. M. (1987). World-view conflict and toddler malnutrition: change–agent dilemmas. In: *Child Survival*, ed. N. Scheper-Hughes, pp. 293–324. Dordrecht: Reidel.

Cleland, J. and van Ginneken, J. K. (1988). Maternal education and child survival in developing countries. The search for pathways of influence. *Social Science and Medicine*, **27**, 1357–68.

Cole, T. J. (1990). The LMS method for constructing normalized growth standards. *European Journal of Clinical Nutrition*, **44**, 45–60.

Cole, T. J. (1993). Seasonal effects on physical growth and development. In: *Seasonality and Human Ecology*, ed. S. J. Ulijaszek and S. Strickland, pp. 89–106. Cambridge: Cambridge University Press.

Dean, A. G., Dean, J. A., Burton, A. H. and Dicker, R. C. (1990). *Epi-Info,*

*Version 5: A word processing, database, and statistics program for epidemiology on micro-computers.* Atlanta, Georgia: Centers for Disease Control.

Dettwyler, K. A. (1992). Infant feeding practices and growth. *Annual Review of Anthropology*, **21**, 171–204.

Diaham, B. and Prentice, A. (1993). Are modern British children too inactive? *British Medical Journal*, **306**, 998–9.

Draper, P. (1976). Social and economic constraints on child life among the !Kung. In: *Kalahari Hunter–Gatherers*, ed. R. Lee and I. DeVore, pp. 199–217. Cambridge, MA: Harvard University Press.

Dressler, W. W. (1995). Modeling biocultural interactions: examples from studies of stress and cardiovascular disease. *Yearbook of Physical Anthropology*, **38**, 27–56.

Ekberg, K. and Mjaavatn, P. E. (eds). (1993). *Children at Risk: Selected Papers.* Trondheim, Norway: The Norwegian Centre for Child Research.

Engle, P. L. and Nieves, I. (1993). Intra-household food distribution among Guatemalan families in a supplementary feeding program: behavior patterns. *Social Science and Medicine*, **36**, 1605–12.

Engle, P. L., Castle, S. and Menon, P. (1996). Child development: vulnerability and resilience. *Social Science and Medicine*, **43**, 621–35.

Flinn, M. V. and England, B. G. (1995). Childhood stress and family environment. *Current Anthropology*, **36**, 854–66.

Flinn, M. W. and England, B. G. (1997). Social economics of childhood glucocorticoid stress response and health. *American Journal of Physical Anthropology*, **102**, 33–53.

Flinn, M. V., Quinlan, R. J., Decker, S. A., Turner, M. T. and England, B. G. (1996). Male–female differences in effects of parental absence on glucocorticoid stress response. *Human Nature*, **7**, 125–62.

Frisancho, A. R. (1993). *Human Adaptation and Accommodation* (enlarged edition). Ann Arbor: The University of Michigan.

Fyfe, A. (1985). *All Work and No Play – Child Labour Today.* A TUC resource book, UNICEF. London: Trades Union Congress.

Garmezy, N. (1983). Stressors of childhood. In: *Stress, Coping and Development in Children*, ed. N. Garmezy and M. Rutter, pp. 43–84. New York: McGraw-Hill.

Gittelsohn, J. (1991). Opening the box: intrahousehold food allocation in rural Nepal. *Social Science and Medicine*, **33**, 1141–54.

Gopalam, C. (1983). Small is Healthy? For the Poor, Not for the Rich. *Nutrition Foundation of India Bulletin*, October.

Gray, S. J. (1998). Butterfat feeding in early infancy in African populations: new hypotheses. *American Journal of Human Biology*, **10** (in press).

Hamill, P. V. V., Drizd, T. A., Johnson, C. L., Reed, R. B., Roche, A. F. and Moore, W. M. (1979). Physical growth: National Center for Health Statistics percentiles. *American Journal of Clinical Nutrition*, **32**, 607–29.

Hansluwka, H. E. (1985). Measuring the health of populations: indicators and interpretations. *Social Science and Medicine*, **20**, 1207–24.

Harrison, G. A. (1993). *Human Adaptation.* Biosocial Society Series (no. 6). Oxford: Oxford Science Publications.

Harrison, G. A., Brush, G., Almedom, A. and Jewell, T. (1990). Short-term variations in stature growth in Ethiopian and English children. *Annals of Human Biology*, **17**, 407–16.

Harrison, G. A., Tanner, J. M., Pilbeam, D. R. and Baker, P. T. (1988). *Human Biology*, 3rd edn. Oxford: Oxford University Press.

Hewlett, B. S. (1991). Demography and childcare in preindustrial societies. *Journal of Anthropological Research*, **47**, 1–37.

Hobcraft, J. N., McDonald, J. W. and Rutstein, S. O. (1983). Child-spacing effects on infant and early child mortality. *Population Index*, **49**, 585–618.

Hobcraft, J. N., McDonald, J. W. and Rutstein, S. O. (1984). Socio-economic factors in infant and child mortality: a cross-national comparison. *Population Studies*, **38**, 193–223.

Hobcraft, J. N., McDonald, J. W. and Rutstein, S. O. (1985). Demographic determinants of infant and early child mortality: a comparative analysis. *Population Studies*, **39**, 363–85.

Huss, A. R. and Ashmore, R. (1996). Issues in the measurement of energy intake for free-living human populations. *American Journal of Human Biology*, **8**, 159–67.

Johnston, F. E. (1995). Environmental constraints on growth: extent and significance. In: *Essays on Auxology*, ed. R. Hauspie, G. Lindgren and F. Falkner, pp. 375–86. Welwyn Garden City: Castlemead Publications.

Kağitçibaşi, Ç. (1996). Family and Human Development Across Cultures – A View from the Other Side. Mahwah, NJ: Lawrence Erlbaum Associates.

Kennedy, E. and Peters, P. (1992). Household food security and child nutrition: the impact of income and gender of household head. *World Development*, **20**, 1077–85.

Koster, F. T., Palmer, D. L., Chakraborty, J., Jackson, T. and Curin, G. (1987). Cellular immune competence and diarrheal morbidity in malnourished Bangladeshi children: a prospective field study. *American Journal of Clinical Nutrition*, **46**,115–20.

Lampl, M. (1993). Evidence of saltatory growth in infancy. *American Journal of Human Biology*, **5**, 641–52.

Lampl, M. and Johnson, M. L. (1997). Identifying saltatory growth patterns in infancy: a comparison of results based on measurement protocol. *American Journal of Human Biology*, **9**, 343–55.

Lawrence, F., Lamb, W. H., Lamb, C. and Lawrence, M. (1985). A quantification of childcare and infant care-giver interaction in a West African village. *Early Human Development*, **12**, 71–80.

Livingstone, M. B. E., Coward, W. A., Prentice, A. M., Davies, P. S. W.,

Strain, J. J., McKenna, P. G., Mahoney, C. A., White, J. A., Stewart, C. M. and Kerr, M. J. (1992). Daily energy expenditure in free-living children: comparison of heart-rate monitoring with the doubly labelled water ($^2$H$_2$$^{18}$O) method. *American Journal of Clinical Nutrition*, **56**, 343–52.

Leonard, W. R. (1989). Nutritional determinants of high-altitude growth in Nuñoa, Peru. *American Journal of Physical Anthropology*, **80**, 341–52.

Leonard, W. R. and Thomas, R. B. (1989). Biosocial responses to seasonal food stress in highland Peru. *Human Biology*, **61**, 65–85.

Lewis, G. (1993). Some studies of social causes of and cultural response to disease. In: *The Anthropology of Disease*, ed. C. G. N. Mascie-Taylor, pp. 73–124. Oxford: Oxford University Press.

Long, B. L., Ungpakorn, G. and Harrison, G. A. (1993). Home–school differences in stress hormone levels in a group of Oxford primary school children. *Journal of Biosocial Science*, **25**, 73–8.

Malina, R. M. (1992). Physical activity and behavioural development during childhood and youth. In: *Physical Activity and Health*, ed. N. G. Norgan, pp. 101–20. Cambridge: Cambridge University Press.

Malina, R. M. (1995). Physical activity and fitness of children and youth: questions and implications. *Medicine, Exercise, Nutrition and Health*, **4**, 123–35.

Malville, N. J. and Malville, J. M. (1996). *Commercial portering of very heavy loads in Eastern Nepal. American Journal of Human Biology*, **8**, 122.

Martorell, R. (1989). Body size, adaptation and function. *Human Organization*, **48**, 15–20.

Martorell, R., Kettel Khan, L. and Schroeder, D. G. (1994). Reversibility of stunting: epidemiological findings in children from developing countries. *European Journal of Clinical Nutrition*, **48** (Suppl. 1), S45–S57.

Mascie-Taylor, C. G. N. (1991). Nutritional status: its measurement and relation to health. In: *Applications of Biological Anthropology to Human Affairs*, ed. C. G. N. Mascie-Taylor and G. W. Lasker, pp. 55–82. Cambridge: Cambridge University Press.

Mosley, W. H. and Chen, L. C. (1984). An analytical framework for the study of child survival in developing countries. In: *Child Survival: Strategies for Research*, ed. W. H. Mosley and L. C. Chen, pp. 25–45. New York: Cambridge University Press.

Nabarro, D. (1984). Social, economic, health and environmental determinants of nutritional status. *Food and Nutrition Bulletin*, **6**, 18–32.

Nabarro, D. and Chinnock, P. (1988). Growth monitoring – inappropriate promotion of an appropriate technology. *Social Science and Medicine*, **26**, 941–8.

Nag, M., White, B. and Peet, R. C. (1978). An anthropological approach to the study of the economic value of children in Java and Nepal. *Current Anthropology*, **19**, 292–306.

Newell, K. W. and Nabarro, D. (1989). Reduced infant mortality: a societal indicator, an emotional imperative, or a health objective? *Transactions of the Royal Society of Tropical Medicine and Hygiene*, **83**, 33–5.

Nieuwenhuys, O. (1994). *Children's Lifeworlds – Gender, Welfare and Labour in the Developing World.* London: Routledge.

Panter-Brick, C. (1992). Women's working behaviour and maternal–child health in rural Nepal. In: *Physical Activity and Health*, ed. N. Norgan, pp. 190–206. Cambridge: Cambridge University Press.

Panter-Brick, C. (1995). Child-care strategies in Nepal: responses to ecology, demography and society. In: *Human Populations: Diversity and Adaptation*, ed. A. J. Boyce and V. Reynolds, pp. 174–88. Oxford: Oxford University Press.

Panter-Brick, C. (1997). Seasonal growth patterns in rural Nepali children. *Annals of Human Biology*, **24**, 1–18.

Panter-Brick, C., Todd, A. and Baker, R. (1996a). Growth status of homeless Nepali boys: do they differ from rural and urban controls? *Social Science and Medicine*, **43**, 441–51.

Panter-Brick, C., Todd, B. A., Baker, R. and Worthman, C. (1996b). Heart rate monitoring of physical activity among village, school and homeless Nepali boys. *American Journal of Human Biology*, **8**, 661–72.

Panter-Brick, C., Worthman, C., Lunn, P., Baker, R. and Todd, A. (1996c). *Urban–rural and class differences in biological markers of stress among Nepali children. American Journal of Human Biology*, **8**, 126.

Pelto, G. H. (1984). Intrahousehold food distribution patterns. In: *Malnutrition: Determinants and Consequences*, ed. P. L. White and N. Selvey, pp. 285–93. New York: Alan R. Liss.

Pollard, A. H., Yusuf, F. and Pollard, G. N. (1974). *Demographic Techniques.* Pergamon Press, Australia.

Pollard, T. (1995). Use of cortisol as a stress marker: practical and theoretical problems. *American Journal of Human Biology*, **7**, 265–74.

Pollitt, E. (ed.). (1995). The relationship between undernutrition and behavioral development in children. *Journal of Nutrition*, **125** (Suppl.), 2211S–2284S.

Prentice, A. and Prentice, A. (1988). Reproduction against the odds. *New Scientist*, **118**, 42–6.

Riddoch, C. J. and Boreham, C. A. G. (1995). The health-related physical activity of children. *Sports Medicine*, **19**, 86–102.

Rowland, M. G. M., Paul, A., Prentice, A. M., Muller, E., Hutton, M., Barrell, R. A. E. and Whitehead, R. G. (1981). In: *Seasonal Dimensions to Rural Poverty*, ed. R. Chambers, R. Longhurst and A. Pacey, pp. 164–75. London: Frances Pinter.

Saul, H. (1994). Fine young slobs? *New Scientist*, **23**, 24–5 (April).

Scheper-Hughes, N. (1991). Social indifference to child death. *Lancet*, **337**, 1144–7.

Scrimshaw, N. S. and Young, V. R. (1989). Adaptation to low protein and energy intakes. *Human Organization*, **48**, 20–30.

Seckler, D. (1982). Small but healthy? A basic hypothesis in the theory, measurement and policy of malnutrition. In: *Newer Concepts in Nutrition and Their Implications for Policy*, ed. P. V. Sukhatme, pp. 127–37. Pune, India: Maharashtra Association for the Cultivation of Science Research Institute.

Shell-Duncan, B. (1993). Cell-mediated immunocompetence among nomadic Turkana children. *American Journal of Human Biology*, **5**, 225–35.

Shell-Duncan, B. (1997). Evaluation of infection and nutritional status as determinants of cellular immunosuppression. *American Journal of Human Biology*, **9**, 381–90.

Shell-Duncan, B. and Wood, J. W. (1997). The evaluation of delayed-type hypersensitivity responsiveness and nutritional status as predictors of gastro-intestinal and acute respiratory infection: a prospective field study among traditional nomadic Kenyan children. *Journal of Tropical Pediatrics*, **43**, 25–32.

Stinson, S. (1980). Child growth and the economic value of children in rural Bolivia. *Human Ecology*, **8**, 89–103.

Sorensen, E. S. (1993). *Children's Stress and Coping: A Family Perspective*. New York: Guilford Press.

Spurr, B. G. and Reina, J. C. (1988). Influence of dietary intervention on artificially increased activity in marginally undernourished Colombian boys. *European Journal of Clinical Nutrition*, **42**, 835–46.

Spurr, B. G. and Reina, J. C. (1990). Daily pattern of %$\dot{V}O_2$max and heart rates in normal and undernourished school children. *Medicine and Science in Sports and Exercise*, **22**, 643–52.

Spurr, G. B., Reina, J. C. and Barac-Nieto, M. (1986). Marginal malnutrition in school-aged Colombian boys: metabolic rate and estimated daily energy expenditure. *American Journal of Clinical Nutrition*, **44**, 113–26.

Super, C. M. and Harkness, S. (1986). The developmental niche: a conceptualization at the interface of child and culture. *International Journal of Behavioral Development*, **9**, 545–69.

Tanner, J. M. (1986). Growth as mirror of the condition of society; secular trends and class distinctions. In: *Human Growth, A Multidisciplinary Review*, ed. A. Demirjian, pp. 3–34. New York: Plenum Press.

Tanner, J. M. and Preece, M. A. (1989). *The Physiology of Human Growth*. Cambridge: Cambridge University Press.

Thomas, R. B. (1976). Energy flow at high altitude. In: *Man in the Andes: A Multi-disciplinary Study of High Altitude Qechua*, ed. P. T. Baker and M. A. Little, pp. 379–404. Stroudsburg, PA: Dowden, Hutchinson and Ross.

Tilford, S. (1995). Promoting the health of the world's children. In: *Childhood to Adolescence – Caring for Health*, ed. A. Fatchett, pp. 241–67. London: Ballière Tindall.

Tomkins, A. M., Dunn, D. T., Hayes, R. J. and Bradley, K. (1986a). Seasonal variations in the nutritional status of urban Gambian children. *British Journal of Nutrition*, **56**, 533–43.

Tomkins, A. M., Hayes, R. J., Dunn, D. T. and Pickering, H. (1986b). Socioeconomic factors associated with child growth in two seasons in an urban Gambian community. *Ecology of Food and Nutrition*, **18**, 107–16.

Ulijaszek, S. J. (1993). Seasonality of reproductive performance in rural Gambia. In *Seasonality and Human Ecology*, ed. S. J. Ulijaszek and S. Strickland, pp. 76–88. Cambridge: Cambridge University Press.

Ulijaszek, S. J. and Strickland, S. S. (1993). *Nutritional Anthropology – Prospects and Perspectives*. London: Smith-Gordon.

UNICEF. (1996). *The State of the World's Children*. 50th Anniversary Issue. Oxford: Oxford University Press.

United Nations. (1993). *ACC/SCN Second Report on the World Nutrition Situation*, vol. II. United Nations.

Waterlow, J. C. (1985). What do we mean by adaptation? In: *Nutritional Adaptation in Man*, ed. K. Blaxter and J. C. Waterlow, pp. 1–11. London and Paris: John Libbey.

Waterlow, J. C. (1988). Preface. In: *Linear Growth Retardation in Less Developed Countries*, ed. J. C. Waterlow, Nestlé Nutrition Workshop Series, vol. 14. New York: Raven Press.

Weiner, M. (1991). *The Child and the State in India – Child Labor and Education Policy in Comparative Perspective*. Princeton, NJ: Princeton University Press.

Weisner, T. S. (1982). Sibling interdependence and child caretaking: a cross-cultural view. In: *Sibling Relationships: Their Nature and Significance Across the Lifespan*, ed. M. E. Lamb and B. Sutton-Smith, pp. 305–27. Hillsdale, NJ: Erlbaum.

Werner, E. E. (1993). Risk, resilience and recovery: perspectives from the Kauai Longitudinal Study. *Development and Psychopathology*, **5**, 503–15.

WHO. (1992). *World Health Statistics Annual, 1991.*World Health Organization. Geneva: Switzerland.

WHO Working Group. (1986). Use and interpretation of anthropometric indicators of nutritional status. *Bulletin of the World Health Organization*, **64**, 929–41.

Woodhead, M. (1990). Psychology and the cultural construction of children's needs. In: Constructing and Deconstructing Childhood: New Directions in the Sociological Study of Childhood, ed. A. James and A. Prout, pp. 60–77. London: Falmer Press.

Zemel, B., Worthman, C. and Jenkins, C. (1993). Differences in endocrine status associated with urban–rural patterns of growth and maturation in Bundi (Gende-speaking) adolescents of Papua New Guinea. In: *Urban Ecology and Health in the Third World*, ed. L. M. Schell, M. T. Smith and A. Bilsborough, pp. 38–60. Cambridge: Cambridge University Press.

# 5

## Child psychology and anthropology: an environmental view

ROBERT A. LEVINE

## Introduction

This chapter provides an overview of major themes and findings in the psychology and anthropology of childhood during the twentieth century, focusing on the nature–nurture problem and its reformulation in the light of contemporary evidence. The study of children and their development is related to, and should involve, numerous disciplines in the biomedical and social sciences. In fact, however, most research on normal child development is conducted and published by psychologists who, together with a smaller number of psychiatrists, also constitute the major influence on what parents, teachers and policy-makers know and think about children in the English-speaking world. As child psychology expanded into a large research field during the 1960s, it lost many of its previously significant connections with the social sciences, and recent anthropological work on children has attempted to revive a cross-cultural dimension to the psychological understanding of children. This changing relation between child psychology and anthropology is a central concern of this chapter.

## An historical overview

The growth of child psychology as a research discipline, and the place of anthropology in it, can be illustrated by the successive editions of *The Manual of Child Psychology*, originally edited as a lengthy one-volume work by Leonard Carmichael in 1946; its chapters reviewed research in the field and included one by Margaret Mead on anthropology ('Research on Primitive Children'). The second edition, in 1954, was also published as one volume and included the same chapter by Margaret Mead(!) with an updated bibliography. The third edition, in 1970, entitled *Carmichael's Manual of Child Psychology* and edited as a two-volume work by Paul Mussen, included a chapter by me, 'Cross-Cultural Study in Child Psychology'. The fourth edition, in 1984, also edited by Paul Mussen, was a four-volume work with a chapter by the Laboratory of Comparative Human Cognition (Michael Cole and colleagues) on culture and cognition. In the fifth edition, now called *The Handbook of Child Psychology* and edited by William Damon in 1997, there are five volumes, but once again only one chapter representing anthropological work ('The Cultural Psychology of Development' by Richard A. Shweder et al.). Thus, the field has grown enormously but the place of anthropology in it has remained small and circumscribed. Other major compendia such as *The Handbook of Infant Development* (Osofsky, 1987) contain no anthropological chapters at all.

The term 'child' is used in psychology to refer to immature offspring from birth up to but not including adolescence, which is recognised as the subject of a different subfield of developmental psychology. The term 'infant' usually means the first 12–24 months after birth; 'young children' as a term is roughly equivalent to the 'pre-school' period, including infancy but also toddlerhood and beyond to 5 years; 'middle childhood' from about 6–10 years of age, after which 'puberty', 'pre-adolescence' and 'early adolescence' take over as developmental terms. Psychologists are aware of the crude and arbitrary nature of these age categories as actual periods of ontogeny, but researchers tend to specialise in a particular period.

The psychological development of children emerged as a topic of scientific interest towards the end of the nineteenth century when the schooling of children became universal in Western Europe and North America and it was thought that science might help understand and improve educational processes. G. Stanley Hall initiated

the 'child study movement' in the USA at the turn of the century
and shortly thereafter Alfred Binet devised the first intelligence tests
for school children in France. During the following nine decades,
child psychology has been heavily North American, extremely
empirical and almost always influenced by European theorists, e.g.
Francis Galton, I. P. Pavlov, Sigmund Freud, Jean Piaget, L. S.
Vygotsky and John Bowlby. In the middle part of the twentieth
century (roughly 1935–60), Clark L. Hull's 'learning theory', a synthesis of the behaviouristic theories of Pavlov and E. L. Thorndike,
dominated psychological research on children. Learning was conceptualised as the formation of habits – invisible but highly predict-
able bonds between environmental stimuli and behavioural
responses – that could be understood best through controlled
experiments on white rats. The principles of habit formation gener-
ated from animal studies were applied to human children. Learning
theory was applied to all kinds of behavioural change, including
those posited by Freud, although it relegated the internal processing
mechanisms, or mental processes – including cognition, language
and conscious experience – to a 'black box' intervening between
stimulus and response that was inaccessible to direct observation
and measurement (Miller and Dollard, 1941; Hull, 1943). This
approach constrained child development research, which focused
on how 'rewards' in the child's environment contributed to the
formation of habits by selective reinforcement of the child's
responses. Questions of how to identify the rewards (or reinforcers)
in childhood environments outside the laboratory were never satis-
factorily answered. Learning theory was not developmental in the
sense of being linked to age-related phases and processes of human
ontogenesis such as the maturation of the central nervous system
in childhood, and its reductionist approach precluded the model-
ling of complex developmental processes. The ideal of child development research as an empirical science using quantitative methods
to test hypotheses was forged during this period and remains with
the field today, but discoveries attributable to behaviouristic child
psychology were few and far between.

  After 1960 the 'cognitive revolution', stimulated by Piaget's
stages of cognitive development, Noam Chomsky's Cartesian model

of language acquisition and artificial intelligence research (the use of computers to model mental processes), brought child psychology out of the animal laboratory and back to its interests in the maturation of children's intellectual capacities. The concept of development was taken seriously as a complex and universal set of processes, with the cognitive maturation of the child as its driving force. Subsequent trends have introduced models and methods from European ethology, behavioural genetics, Bowlby's attachment theory and sociolinguistics, balancing the focus on cognition with an equal emphasis on social and emotional development.

The findings from child development research since 1960 cannot be summarised briefly (Damon's 1997 handbook has five volumes of lengthy summaries) but psychologists have made many discoveries over the last 35 years. They have charted the emergence of the child's capacities (cognitive, communicative, emotional and social) and their growth and transformation over the period from birth to adolescence. As the result of their efforts, we now know a great deal about what kinds of experience children of different ages are *capable* of having and responding to, even when we do not know what experiences they actually have in the diverse environments of human societies. Infant psychologists have demonstrated, for example, that humans at birth have remarkable capacities for perception, cognition (including memory), emotional arousal, learning and social responsiveness, and that these capacities grow rapidly during the first year of life – contradicting earlier concepts of human infants as mentally incompetent. These scientific achievements are fundamental to the understanding of child development. One weakness of child psychology lies in its tendency to generalise to the human species as a whole without considering the narrow range of environmental contexts in which most of its empirical observations are made, a problem that has dogged the field from its beginnings (Whiting, 1954). This is where anthropology comes in.

Anthropology has played a distinctive but limited role in the history of child psychology, as a gadfly deflating universal claims concerning human psychological development, as a growing body of evidence on childhood environments outside the Western world and as a basis for environmentalist positions in the nature–nurture debate. Margaret Mead's *Coming of Age in Samoa*, published in 1928, challenged G. Stanley Hall's formulation of adolescent turmoil as universal and established the role of evidence from non-Western societies as relevant to the acceptance or rejection of universal generalisation about human development. Sometimes derided by psychologists as 'the anthropological veto', this role remains an important way for anthropology to contribute to the understanding of childhood, especially as psychologists persist in making universal claims without cross-cultural evidence to support them. In 1930, Mead's *Growing Up in New Guinea*, based on her field work in Manus (in the Admiralty Islands just north of New Guinea), provided our first ethnographic description of the lives of young children in a non-Western society; she also challenged Piaget's ideas about moral development in childhood on the basis of her Manus field work (Mead, 1932). Mead's early work was followed in the next decade by other anthropological field studies of children and child rearing, including those of Meyer Fortes (1938) in Africa, John W. M. Whiting (1941) in New Guinea, Gregory Bateson and Mead (1942) in Bali and Jules and Zunia Henry (1944) in South America. The analysis of child training practices in 75 societies by Whiting and Child (1953) demonstrated that the archives of anthropological publications already contained a substantial amount of ethnographic evidence on the lives of children in different parts of the world, collected not by specialists in the field but by general ethnographers, including missionaries, who included material on children in their monographs concerning the culture of a particular community. These were not psychologically sophisticated accounts, but they afforded much more than the adults' view of childhood, including the interpersonal experience of children at different ages and stages, the tasks they learned and performed, the games they played and the ways in which they participated in the community. Barry and Paxson (1971) later provided a body of coded data on child rearing from published ethnographic descriptions in 186 societies.

The Six Cultures Study (B. Whiting, 1963; J. Whiting et al., 1966; Whiting and Whiting, 1975; Whiting and Edwards, 1988), launched as a comparative field project in 1954, was a landmark in the anthropological study of childhood, providing extensive descriptions and systematic observations of children's environments and behaviour in rural communities in India, Mexico, Okinawa, the Philippines, Kenya and Massachusetts. The observational data on children 3–11 years old were analysed comparatively to show the impact of spatial and social structures on children's relationships and activities (Whiting and Whiting, 1975) and the differentiation of behaviour by gender in childhood (Whiting and Edwards, 1988). The Whitings and their collaborators were committed to the eclectic programme of ethnography common to anthropological community studies of the 1950s, and the large body of evidence collected could be examined in ecological, cultural, developmental, behavioural and psychodynamic terms.

Anthropologists and psychologists trained by the Whitings at Harvard went on to conduct studies inspired by the Six Cultures Study in Kenya (e.g. Munroe and Munroe, 1971; Harkness and Super, 1977; Leiderman and Leiderman, 1977; Super and Harkness, 1982; Weisner, 1989; Wenger, 1989; LeVine et al., 1994) and a variety of other places, for example Botswana (Konner, 1972), Guatemala (Rogoff, 1990, 1993), Liberia (Erchak, 1980) and India (Seymour, 1975). The evidence on childhood in diverse cultures has continued to grow, but at a slow rate; a relatively small number of anthropologists, development psychologists and linguists have conducted such studies over the past 30 years.

As the result of publications following the expansion of anthropological research all over the world since 1960, we know a great deal about the lives and environments of children in diverse cultures, even though specialised developmental studies have been relatively few. Some findings are summarised below. When they are invoked in theoretical discussions of child development, it is usually – from Margaret Mead in 1928 to the present – to support an environmentalist perspective in which cross-population variations in the conditions under which children grow up are interpreted as affecting their acquisition of language, behavioural characteristics and psychological dispositions. This interpretation of the evidence bears on the long-standing, politically charged, controversies over the relative importance of innate and acquired factors in educational performance, occupational achievement, personal character and mental illness: the nature–nurture debate.

## Nature and nurture

The idea of an opposition between 'nature' and 'nurture' in the formation of character has a long history in Anglo-American culture: In *The Tempest*, Prospero characterises Caliban as:

> A devil, a born devil, on whose nature
> Nurture can never stick; on whom my pains,
> Humanely taken, all, all lost, quite lost . . .

In this play of 1612 Shakespeare assumes that his audience will understand the distinction between nature and nurture as formative influences on moral character, and he formulates – in terms that still resonate – the complaint by someone of privilege that inborn unworthiness in the disadvantaged renders efforts at improvement futile. Of course, it was Francis Galton (1869), more than 250 years after Shakespeare, who launched the scientific debate about nature and nurture (using those terms) as determinants of mental capacities, and since then the pendulum of educated opinion has swung back and forth, frequently pushed to extremes by intensely political controversies over eugenics, Nazi racism, Soviet Lysenkoism and the struggles for and against racial equality.

Ironically, biological scientists of different persuasions agreed in principle decades ago that genetic and environmental factors should be seen as interacting and collaborating in the individual development of humans rather than as opposed sets of potentially dominant explanatory factors. This consensus remains in place among geneticists (Plomin et al., 1990), but it has not prevented others from taking strong positions in favour of nature *or* nurture. The last few years have seen the emergence in the USA of a 'new innatism' claiming that equalitarian bias among psychologists and social scientists has led them to adopt cultural and other environmental explanations of child development while failing to recognise growing evidence of genetic influence (Degler, 1991; Scarr, 1992).

According to this view, child development researchers are so afraid that acknowledgement of genetic influence will lead them to be accused of racism that they take 'politically correct' environmentalist positions even on issues where the evidence points unmistakably in the opposite direction. This is portrayed as being especially misguided at a time when every week brings news of findings that link genes with behaviour.

There have in fact been great advances in our knowledge of human heredity, environments and child development in recent years, but it is mainly those concerning heredity that are widely publicised. Indeed, the discoveries of molecular genetics, evolutionary biology and neuroscience have propelled those areas to the forefront of scientific progress in our time. Their breakthroughs have created, particularly in the press but also among some scientists, an excitement that is not matched in the social sciences, an impatience with the complexities and uncertainties of social inquiry, and an expectation that the normal as well as abnormal behaviours of children and adults will soon be explained in terms of genes. In this climate it is not surprising that inflated claims of genetic determination are uncritically accepted, particularly as the excesses of earlier environmentalist trends (for example, blaming parents for their children's mental ills and disabilities) have diminished the credibility of environmentalism.

Recent genetic determinist positions concerning child development (Scarr, 1992), however understandable they may be as a corrective to past fallacies, do not stand up to close examination for three reasons. First, geneticists have not actually identified any gene that controls normal psychological variation in the human species and it is not clear when they will be able to do so (Mann, 1994). At the moment, the strongest evidence for genetic influence on normal behaviour (as opposed to neurological defects and other pathologies), and that most cited by innatists, comes largely from expanded replications of psychological studies that were conducted many years ago; their findings are not new and are not a product of molecular biology, neuroscience or other recent advances in biology. Second, the research record in both behavioural genetics and developmental psychology shows that in numerous cases, studies claiming to have found a genetic influence on human behaviour were falsified by subsequent research (Mann, 1994). As a human behavioural geneticist told the *New York Times* recently, 'Our field is littered with failures to replicate' (Angier, 1996). Thus, we are not faced with a uniformly expanding body of knowledge favouring genetic explanations of human behaviour and development. Third, and most importantly, even the best psychological studies on which the innatist position rests were conducted with samples drawn from an extremely restricted range of environments in Western populations, thus inflating the apparent genetic influence. Behavioural geneticists usually mention in their research reports that an estimate of genetic influence (i.e. H, the heritability coefficient) is population-specific and cannot be generalised from one population to another or to the human species as a whole. The most scrupulous investigators go beyond that to emphasise, as Bouchard et al. (1990) did of their findings from the famous Minnesota Twin Study, that they 'should not be extrapolated to the extremes of environmental disadvantage still encountered in society'. (By this they mean that twins separated at birth are not placed in new environments at random but selectively placed in homes judged likely to provide 'good care', thus leaving out the lower socioeconomic strata of American society in which poverty and family disorganisation are common; thus, the results cannot be interpreted as applying to the entire population of the United States or even Minnesota.) Innatist manifestos like *The Bell Curve* (Herrnstein and Murray, 1994) usually make this extrapolation anyway. This is a central flaw in current hereditarian positions, and it is one that an anthropological perspective on child development research can correct.

## The current state of knowledge: a summary formulation

Child development research has provided a new basis for understanding how children experience their environments during the first years after birth. Infant psychology has shown that the newborn child's capacities for sensation, perception, cognition, memory, learning, social engagement and communication are far greater than was imagined before 1960 (Osofsky, 1987; Bates and Elman, 1997). These capacities develop rapidly during the first year of life and register the baby's interaction with stable features of the caregiving environment, providing a basis for the development of social relationships. Before 6 months of age, infants discriminate among the humans in that environment and show their preference for conditions that have given them comfort when distressed. By 12 months, they have definite expectations for interpersonal stimulation and comfort, have become attached to their mothers and others who have interacted with them and have learned some of the conventions of social distance and conversation in their local environment. All of this means that in the first year of life infants are actively learning, participating and forming relationships in a socially structured environment.

The second and third years of life, specifically from 18 to 36 months, constitute the most rapid period of language acquisition when the child becomes capable of speech. Sociolinguists have shown that during this period a great deal more is acquired by the child than the remarkable abilities to pronounce words and form sentences, viz. the conventions of conversation in that culture, the preferred forms of emotional expressiveness and emotional control, and the normative strategies for using speech to serve one's own intentions and other's expressed desires. This is also a period when children form stable gender identities and begin to organise their culturally structured experience around the concept of being male and female. Furthermore, we now know that by 3 years of age children have learned rules reflecting the moral values of their society and have strong feelings about those rules. In other words, the first 3 years of life are extraordinarily busy ones for the child's socialisation and acquisition of culture.

Anthropologists of child rearing from the 1930s onwards assumed that the acquisition of culture began in infancy and described infant care practices in detail (LeVine and Norman, in press), but they were not, even in the 1950s, aware of the infant capacities mentioned above or of the specific channels through which children under 3 years of age learn to participate in social relationships and acquire the rules governing them. The Six Cultures Study, planned and carried out from 1954 to 1957, was no exception. But because these and later studies lacking sophistication in infant psychology provided enthnographic descriptions of the interpersonal environments of children and their parents' ideas and practices, we know a good deal about the social lives of children during the first 3 years as well as later (Shweder et al., 1997). From this sociological and observational research it is possible to draw some general conclusions about childhood in the full range of human societies.

## Cultural variation

Variation across human populations in parental practices and in the behavioural development of young children is wide, unpredictable from knowledge of universal human capacities (in the way that software programs are unpredictable from the hardware that supports them), and extends to aspects of childhood that are 'biologically programmed'. For example, humans are mammals with a highly adaptive capacity for lactation, but breast-feeding is no longer universal in the species because of cultural preferences and the advent of synthetic milk formula. Even where the practice of breast-feeding is the norm, however, its average duration varies widely across human populations from less than a year to 2 years or more. Other variations in childhood environments are mentioned below, but it is worth noting here that even the attainment of motor skills in the first and second years of life (sitting, standing, walking) can be acclerated or slowed down according to the preferences of parents, and this varies not only across culturally distinct populations (who might differ in the genetic basis for these skills) but within the same breeding population according to the social experience (e.g. urbanisation, education) of the parents. Super (1976) found that East African infants exhibiting 'precocious' motor skills had been trained by parents who sought to facilitate the early development of these skills, and that parents of the same ethnic group who were urban and had been to school were less likely to provide this facilitation or to have infants with as early a development of motor skill.

Language development provides insight into how universals and culturally variable particulars fit together. There is a panhuman speech anatomy and a universal maturational schedule for the child's acquisition of a first language during the 18- to 36-month period, but many other aspects of language developments are variable. The particular language itself constitutes a distinctive symbolic environment for the child to master through participation, including the conventional norms and forms of verbal communication with persons of differing social status, and the uses of language to express and conceal feelings (Ochs and Schieffelin, 1984; Schieffelin and Ochs, 1986). The child's acquisition and use of a *culture-specific* code of communication represents a realisation of the universal human capacities for speech.

## Parental goals and concepts

Parental practices and the parents' organisation of the child's environment are goal-driven, and the goals are largely derived from conceptions of care, infancy and childhood embedded in local cultural ideologies. Every culture has a conceptual division of the life course into stages linked roughly or precisely to age and imputed maturational capacities, with associated social responsibilities and stereotypical psychological characteristics. Something equivalent to infancy and childhood stages seem to be universal, although the number of age-linked partitions and their meanings vary considerably. The only claimed exception of which I am aware is medieval Europe as described by Ariès (1962) who maintained that childhood as a distinct stage of life had yet to be discovered. Shahar (1990), however, disputes this contention on the basis of her recent investigation of childhood in Western Europe during the Middle Ages:

> In contrast to Ariès, I believe that childhood was in fact perceived as a distinct stage in the life cycle, that there was a conception of childhood, and that educational theories and norms existed. These norms were broached and formulated by theologians, secular and

ecclesiastical legislators, jurists, the authors of medical and didactic works, and preachers.

(Shahar, 1990: 3)

The authors of medieval didactic literature divided childhood into stages . . . reminiscent of the classifications of Piaget or Erikson.

(Shahar, 1990: 7)

## Caregivers

The care of infants and toddlers in virtually all human populations is the socially assigned responsibility of the biological mother, although she may delegate that responsibility to others on a temporary or permanent basis or even transfer the responsibility to someone else altogether, depending on the norms of her community. Observational studies indicate that supplementary caregivers are most frequently adult women (particularly where several related families share domestic facilities), older siblings of the child (often where adult women do not share facilities) and, much less frequently, fathers and other adult males. Despite the relative rarity of paternal caregivers of children in their early years, there is considerable variation across populations (Hewlett, 1992), and it is possible that additional ethnographic studies in South Asia will provide more examples of paternal care. In some parts of the world, e.g. Micronesia, Sierra Leone and the Caribbean, mothers give their young children to their mothers or other female kin to raise for at least a period of years, and a majority of children under 2 years of age are living with and being cared for by someone other than their mothers. Thus, variation in caregiving personnel, restricted in range, is quite considerable across human societies and there is population-specific patterning in the extent to which caregivers of differing age and sex are available to a child.

## Interaction with other children

Sibling care and child-to-child social interaction are frequent in many societies and form a primary context for learning and the development of relationships during childhood. Fertility is involved here, for where the mother bears five or more children on average and they survive infancy, there are likely to be older siblings living at home when she gives birth. In some cases, as mentioned above, the mother may have no one but her older children to help her with infant care when she is working in cultivation, food processing or trade. In other cases, as in many African societies, there are adult women available and willing to help with day-time care of infants, but their children are also likely to form groups into which the young child is absorbed.

It is important to recognise, as pointed out by Konner (1975), that these groups of siblings and neighbours are not peer groups but multi-age groups of juveniles. Peer groups occur where children are segregated by age, as in the classes of Western-type schools. Where there is no such deliberate segregation, however, the social lives of children and their opportunities to learn differ from those of children in peer groups. Konner proposed that learning is enhanced by a multi-age structure because young children imitate older children more easily than they imitate adults, and it is harder to learn from peers because they are more likely to be at the same level of knowledge and skill. Dunn (1983) argues from a psychological viewpoint that the sibling relationship combines the difference in authority and knowledge of the parent–child relationships with the equality, similarity and ease of interaction of peers, creating a uniquely important social context for the child's development. It seems likely that in communities where sibling caregiving and multi-age groups of children are prevalent, they promote the learning of social responsibility and task competence in young children.

## Schooling

Western-type schools are distinctive in children's lives in more ways than their age-segregation. When compared with the social contexts of learning in communities without schools, other features become clear. In such communities, children learn to master adaptive tasks, but there are no special institutions or settings dedicated to instruction. They learn through participation in economic production and other activities organised by adults, beginning as peripheral participants who perform simple and repetitive tasks while having observational access to the mature practice of their elders (Lave, 1990; Lave and Wenger, 1991). It may be that no one pays attention to them except when they do something wrong; they receive guidance only as corrective feedback. Gradually they progress to more advanced tasks that they have seen others perform. In many agrarian societies where economic production is at home, this process can begin in the second or third year of life and continue up to adolescence; where there is a formal aprenticeship in craft production, the boy may begin at the age of 10 years or older, after having served an informal apprenticeship at home. Schools are specialised institutional settings dedicated to instructional purposes in which an adult expert concerns him or herself exclusively with the education of child novices and communicates with them verbally in a room set aside for that purpose. When children in a community that has previously had no schools begin to attend, their lives become different from those who never went to school in more ways than what they learn and how: they become subject to an authority outside the family and are increasingly connected with a wider social world outside the community.

These five points illustrate the kinds of knowledge we have gained from anthropological research on parenthood and childhood in humans. They indicate variation in many aspects of the child's environment and call for a theory of childhood environments more grounded in the evidence of cultural variations than any yet proposed.

## Environmental optimisation theory

Cross-cultural studies of child rearing are making possible a new view of human childhood, with implications for how we conceptualise the nurture part of the nature–nurture interaction. As E. O. Wilson (1975) stated in *Sociobiology*, population variability in social organisation and social behaviour is a human species characteristic. A systematic population-level analysis, as used in genetics, epidemiology and demography, can integrate evidence from anthropology and other fields of social and biomedical inquiry with those of developmental psychology. As social behaviour and the environments involved in its ontogeny vary widely across human populations of differing geographical locations and historical periods, the statistical and cultural analysis of these variations is essential to the scientific understanding of human behavioural development.

My theory of environmental optimisation, based on findings from comparative studies of human development, is designed to shed light on questions of nature and nurture. It is compatible with modern biology, economics and developmental psychology. The basic tenets of this proposed theory follow, with illustrative examples.

## Optimal development in cultural perspective

Every human population organises the environments of its young around certain developmental priorities for health, skills and virtue that are conceptualised as optimal or desirable in local cultural terms. Our comparison of the Gusii people of Kenya with middle-class North Americans (LeVine et al., 1994) can serve to illustrate this point.

An interdisciplinary team of investigators conducted a 17-month longitudinal study of 28 infants and their families in a Gusii community of rural Kenya, and then collected comparable data on mother–infant interaction at home and in the laboratory among middle-class North American mothers in the Boston area. The conditions of parenthood and infant care among the Gusii that contrast with those of Boston include domestically organised agricultural production, high fertility (an average of nine to 10 children per married woman, compared with a little over two in the USA, moderately high infant mortality (about 80 per 1000 live births in Kenya at the time compared to about 10 in the USA at that time), a tradition of polygynous marriage, and a reliance on children (often older siblings) to take care of infants while mothers work in the fields. Gusii infants are breast-fed for an average of 16 months, sleep with their mothers at night, are carried on the backs of their mothers and child caregivers in the day-time. But Gusii infant care

Table 5.1. *Maternal attention in early child care: quantity and quality*

|  | Gusii: Paediatric model | American: Pedagogical model |
|---|---|---|
| Goal | Protection | Active engagement, social exchange |
| Means | Soothing | Stimulation, protoconversation |
| Temporal distribution over first 30 months | Decreasing | Increasing |
| Cultural script for selective responsiveness | Respond to distress Modulate excitement Commands | Respond to babble Elicit excitement Questions, praise |

*Source:* LeVine et al. (1994: 249).

as a system can only be understood in terms of the cultural model followed by mothers that shape the proximal environments of their offspring over the 2 years of life.

A cultural model, meaning an ethnographic reconstruction of the premises on which the child care practices of a people are based, can be seen as having three parts: a moral direction, a pragmatic design and a set of conventional scripts for action. The moral direction refers to the normative assumptions about what is best for an infant and what the goals are to which mothers and other care-givers should be devoted. The pragmatic design means the general strategy for attaining these goals, specific behavioural devices used and the schedule for their deployment over infancy and early child-hood. The conventional scripts for action are socially expected sequences of caregiving behaviour in specific situations, such as responding to the infant's states and communicative signals, that are considered not only normal but natural and necessary.

The differences between Gusii and North American white middle-class mothers in the kinds and amount of attention they give their infants over the first 30 months of life are summarised schematically as cultural models in Table 5.1. The first column breaks the model down into goals (i.e. moral direction), means and temporal distribution (pragmatic design), and script for responding to infant signals (the conventional script for action). The Gusii model is called paediatric because its primary concern is with the survival, health and physical growth of the infant, and the North American model pedagogical because its primary concern is with the behavioural development of the infant and its preparation for educational interactions. These titles are interpretations of the divergent moral directions of the two models; they represent different ways of construing the problems of infant care and how maternal attention should be allocated towards their solution in two different settings.

The evidence supporting this comparison is provided in a monograph reporting the results (LeVine et al., 1994). It demonstrates that mothers in the two cultures have different practices reflecting contrasting agendas for infant development, that each agenda has a logic (it makes sense as a means towards culturally formulated ends) and an ethic (mothers believe their own practices to be in the best interests of their children), and that maternal behaviour in accordance with culture-specific models results in a distinctive pattern of social and communicative interaction over the course of infancy and early childhood. Thus, a microscopic examination of infant social environments in two different populations reveals a greater divergence of early interactions than universalist models would predict, and it suggests that they constitute alternative pathways for behavioural development consistent with health and growth under varying conditions. The Gusii–American comparison implies that, as the mothers of a particular population follow the culture-specific agenda of a local model of infant care, they selectively facilitate the development of certain potentials and capacities of the child rather than others. Cultural images of maturity entail and elaborate particular goals for a child's development, providing parents with standards for guiding the behavioural development of the child.

## Institutions and resources

As cultural priorities for child development become institutionalised, resources are allocated, recurrently and through multiple channels, to the environmental processes that promote them in children throughout a population. There are microsocial processes involved, as parents of a community pursue their common agenda for the realisation of their children's potential by investing domestic resources (including parental time and attention) in the selective development of children's capacities and later by recruiting sponsors through kin and friendship networks to advance the careers of their children. There may also be macrosocial processes involved, as when the state organises programmes of health and education affecting all children in accordance with national or provincial goals established through political decision-making. Looked at this way, the institutional structure of society at both micro- and macro-levels is implicated in the differential promotion of behavioural development during childhood.

## Priming and precocity

At the microsocial level, the cross-cultural evidence shows parents to be 'priming' their children for the early development of skills considered most useful and virtuous by local standards, so that the children exhibit behaviour in their pre-school years that would be considered precocious in other cultural groups. This can be seen in a preliminary comparison of results from German studies with the findings from the Gusii and North American research. In each case goals for behavioural development formulated in a cultural model are hypothesised to promote the early ('precocious' by the standards of *other* cultures) emergence of a particular behaviour that has been selectively facilitated in infancy and early childhood. The Gusii want children who are respectful, obedient and responsible, in childhood as well as later, and their implementation of the paediatric model outlined on Table 5.1 promotes these virtues in their early stages: babies who cry infrequently and are easily quieted during the first year, who respond obediently to maternal commands as they acquire language comprehension skill and who are able to be responsible babysitters for their infant siblings at the age of 6 years, and sometimes younger. (We also posit a Respect–Obedience model that takes over as the child's survival is assured.)

Their expectations for exciting social interaction are low, compared with North American children, and their ability to fit into the family hierarchy as workers is precocious by North American standards (LeVine et al., 1994).

North American middle-class parents want their offspring to become mature adults who are self-confident and socially engaged, and they set about promoting those virtues during infancy, as the pedagogical model suggests. They involve the infant in social interactions designed not only to be cognitively stimulating and emotionally exciting but also to promote sociability and self-esteem, using reciprocal vocalisation, verbal interaction and frequent questioning and praise as primary methods. The result is children who are talkative and verbally assertive in the pre-school years, precociously so by the standards of other cultures. (Among the Gusii, to call a young child talkative, *omokwani*, is pejorative, implying the child lacks respect.)

In Germany, self-reliance (*selbständigkeit*) is an explicit goal of mature development, but it is interpreted as involving a greater social distance between child and mother than among contemporary North American middle-class parents, who none the less value 'independence' as a developmental goal (Norman, 1991; Harkness et al., 1992; LeVine and Norman, in press). German mothers promote this virtue during infancy by leaving the baby alone in bed on awakening in the morning and at other times when the mother goes out of the house; they also push away a baby who gets 'too close' and refuse to indulge one who cries for companionship, a behaviour they consider indicative of being spoilt, *verwöhnt* (Grossmann and Grossman, 1981; Grossmann et al., 1985; LeVine and Norman, in press). It is noteworthy that these maternal behaviours are considered morally unacceptable among contemporary middle-class North Americans, and certain behaviours, like leaving a baby unattended when the mother goes out shopping, constitute criminal neglect in many states of the USA.

What is the result of the German pattern of infant care? The Grossmanns report that in their Bielefeld sample, the 10-month-old infants observed at home initiated pickup by their mothers less often and took less notice of their comings and goings than in Ainsworth's classic study of infants and mothers in Baltimore, Maryland (Ainsworth et al., 1978). Further comparison was permitted by observation in the Strange Situation, the most widely used method for assessing attachment to the mother in 1-year-old children.

In the Strange Situation, a 12-month-old infant is temporarily separated from the mother in a home-like laboratory setting, and videotaped over a scripted series of eight episodes (Table 5.2). When the mother returns (Episodes 5 and 8), if the child avoids contact with her ('anxious-avoidant', class A) or is inconsolably distressed as the mother tries to comfort him ('anxious-resistant', class C), the child is considered insecurely attached to the mother. The securely attached child (class B) is distressed by the mother's absence but consoled by her comforting when they are reunited.

When the Bielefeld babies were observed in the Strange Situation at 12 months, 49% of them, compared with 26% of the Baltimore infants, were classified as anxious-avoidant (A), meaning they avoided their mother in the reunion episodes (Grossmann et al., 1985). A similar result has been found in East Berlin (Ahnert et al., in press), whereas in most North American studies the proportion of A babies is one-quarter or less. The Grossmanns also report that infants classified as B-3 in the Strange Situation, considered 'optimal' by USA researchers, would be thought spoiled and immature in Germany. There is, in other words, evidence to suggest that German infants are (in a USA–German comparison) precociously capable of self-comforting as opposed to seeking comfort from their mothers, at home and in the Strange Situation, in accordance with their parents' concept of mature behaviour. From the viewpoint of environmental optimisation theory, German children, like their North American and Gusii counterparts, are primed during infancy and early childhood to respond to other persons in ways that their parents consider culturally appropriate. This is the first step in the child's acquisition of culture.

The cultural priming of young children is also evident in Japan (Shwalb and Shwalb, 1996). There a leading parental priority is for children to acquire *omoiyari*, i.e. empathy, interpersonal sensitivity, the ability to anticipate the feelings of others (Lebra, 1976). This

Table 5.2. *Summary of episodes of the Strange Situation*

| Number of episodes | Persons present | Duration | Brief description of action |
|---|---|---|---|
| 1 | Mother, baby, observer | 30 s | Observer introduces mother and baby to experimental room, then leaves |
| 2 | Mother, baby | 3 min | Mother is non-participant while baby explores; if necessary, play is stimulated after 2 min |
| 3 | Stranger, mother, baby | 3 min | Stranger enters. First minute: stranger silent. Second minute: stranger converses with mother. Third minute: stranger approaches baby. After 3 min mother leaves unobtrusively |
| 4 | Stranger, baby | 3 min or less[a] | First separation episode: stranger's behaviour is geared to that of baby |
| 5 | Mother, baby | 3 min or more[b] | First reunion episode: mother greets and/or comforts baby, then tries to settle him/her again in play. Mother then leaves, saying 'bye-bye' |
| 6 | Baby alone | 3 min or less[a] | Second separation episode |
| 7 | Stranger, baby | 3 min or less[a] | Continuation of second separation: stranger enters and gears her behaviour to that of baby |
| 8 | Mother, baby | 3 min | Second reunion episode: mother enters, greets baby, then picks him/her up; meanwhile, stranger leaves unobtrusively |

*Notes:*
[a] Episode is curtailed if the baby is unduly distressed.
[b] Episode is prolonged if more time is required for the baby to become reinvolved in play.
*Source:* Ainsworth et al. (1978: 37).

includes the avoidance of confrontational language and its replacement with indirect patterns of speech, which mothers teach their 2-year-olds (Clancy, 1986), and which 5-year-old Japanese children have been observed using spontaneously to avoid potential confrontations with other children in play settings (Kelly, 1989). Here again, a parental model for development is translated into the child's precocious behaviour, in this case involving what would be thought of elsewhere as a sophisticated strategy of interpersonal diplomacy. Comparing the Japanese with Germans, North Americans and Gusii on the basis of these fragmentary but striking observations, it appears that culture-specific parental preferences – for an empathic, self-reliant, talkative or obedient child, respectively – can accelerate the emergence of behaviour patterns consistent with these goals early in the child's development.

### Cumulative impact

The institutionalisation of developmental priorities gives them a place in social life that lasts beyond one generation, as cultural traditions and ideologies at the microsocial level influencing parental investment, or as macrosocial structures for social participation that affect the welfare and activities of children. The cumulative effects of persistent resource allocations by governments and other macrosocial bureaucratic institutions over the generations can dramatically change population parameters affecting children's lives: for example, fertility, mortality and literacy rates. Mass schooling, health services and family planning programmes, involving macrosocial and microsocial change operating over time, have altered the environments of children, particularly during the twentieth century by moving many populations towards small families with high rates of survival and literacy.

### Heritability

When the population characteristics affecting childhood approach an optimum, for example when the infant mortality rate approaches zero and the literacy rate approaches 100%, as in the most uniformly developed contemporary nations such as Japan and Sweden, these changes entail steep reductions in environmentally caused variations in these rates, and the population-specific heritabilities of mortality and illiteracy are correspondingly increased. In other words, when policy measures have virtually eliminated inequality in the environmental sources of these developmental outcomes while leaving the genetic sources unchanged, genes become more important than environmental factors as determinants of infant mortality and illiteracy. Within such national populations, and in subnational populations defined by caste and class (e.g. the North American white middle class), narrowing the range of environmental variations through social policy has elevated the relative genetic contribution to problematic outcomes (such as infant deaths or inability to read) and given public salience to genetic problems. Thus, estimating the relative contributions of genes and environments to policy-influenced developmental outcomes involving health and education on the basis of research in the most developed or 'optimised' populations inevitably overestimates the genetic contribution.

## Conclusion

This theoretical model of environmental optimisation as an historical process has implications for the comparative analysis of variations in behavioural development across populations at all levels, national and subnational, and for attempts to explain such variations in terms of genetic and environmental influences. When societies in the course of their historical development have adopted a goal of human development like improving the health and education of all their children and have invested resources in it over several generations, it has been possible to eradicate the environmental obstacles to those goals to a degree that could hardly have been predicted in the middle of the nineteenth century. A worldwide historical perspective shows the overwhelming power of social forces to transform the conditions of child development, altering parameters of reproduction and parental care that had been in place for many centuries. These macrosocial processes are as relevant to children as the microsocial ones psychologists and anthropologists study, and they indicate the need for a social science of child development concerned with the environments of children throughout the world.

## References

Ahnert, L., Meischner, T., Zeibe, M. and Schmidt, A. (in press). Socialization concepts of Russian and German mothers in infant caretaking. In: *The Organization of Attachment Relationships: Maturation, Culture and Context*, ed. P. M. Crittenden. New York: Cambridge University Press.

Ainsworth, M. D. S., Blehar, M., Waters, E. and Wall, S. (1978). *Patterns of Attachment: A Psychological Study of the Strange Situation*. Hillsdale, NJ: Lawrence Erlbaum Associates.

Angier, N. (1996). Maybe it's not a gene behind a person's thrill-seeking ways. *New York Times*, November 1, 1996, A22.

Ariès, P. (1962). *Centuries of Childhood: A Social History of Family Life*. Translated from the French by Robert Baldick. New York: Random House.

Barry, H. III and Paxson, L. (1971). Infancy and early childhood: cross-cultural codes 2. *Ethnology*, **10**, 466–508.

Bates, E. and Elman, J. (1997). Learning rediscovered (research on language learning by infants). *Science*, **274**, 1849–50.

Bateson, G. and Mead, M. (1942). *Balinese Character: A Photographic Analysis*. New York: New York Academy of Sciences.

Bouchard, T., Lykken, D., McGue, M., Segal, N. and Tellegen, A. (1990). Sources of human psychological differences: the Minnesota study of twins reared apart. *Science*, **250**, 223–8.

Carmichael, L. (ed.) (1944). *Manual of Child Psychology*. New York: John Wiley.

Clancy, P. (1986). The acquisition of communicative style in Japanese. In: *Language Socialization Across Cultures*, ed. B. Schieffelin and E. Ochs. New York: Cambridge University Press.

Damon, W. (ed.). (1997). *Handbook of Child Psychology*, vols I–V. New York: John Wiley.

Degler, C. N. (1991). *Search of Human Nature: The Decline and Revival of Darwinism in American Social Thought*. New York: Oxford University Press.

Dunn, J. (1983). Sibling relationships in early childhood. *Child Development*, **54**, 787–811.

Erchak, G. M. (1980). The acquisition of cultural rules by Kpelle children. *Ethos*, **8**, 40–8.

Fortes, M. (1938). *Social and Psychological Aspects of Education in Taleland*. London: Oxford University Press.

Grossmann, K. and Grossman, K. E. (1991). Newborn behavior, the quality of early parenting and later toddler–parent relationships in a group of German infants. In: *The Cultural Context of Infancy*, vol. 2, ed. J. K. Nugent, B. M. Lester and T. B. Brazelton. Norwood, NJ: Ablex.

Grossmann, K., Grossman, K. E., Spangler, G., Suess, G. and Unzner, L. (1985). Maternal sensitivity and newborns' orientation responses as related to quality of attachment in northern Germany. In: *Growing Points of Attachment Theory and Research*, ed. I. Bretherton and E. Waters. Monographs of the Society for Research in Child Development, vol. 50, Nos 1–2. Chicago: University of Chicago Press.

Grossmann, K. E. and Grossman, K. (1981). Parent–infant attachment relationships in Bielefeld. In: *Behavioral Development: The Bielefeld Interdisciplinary Project*, ed. K. Immelman, G. Barlow, L. Petrovich and M. Main. New York: Cambridge University Press.

Harkness, S. and Super, C. (1977). Why African children are so hard to test. In: *Issues in Cross-Cultural Research*, ed. L. Adler. New York: *Annals of the New York Academy of Sciences*, **285**, 326–31.

Harknss, S, Super, C. and Keefer, C. H. (1992). Learning to be an American parent: how cultural models gain directive force. In: *Human Motives and Cultural Models*, ed. R. D'Andrade and C. Strauss. New York: Cambridge University Press.

Henry, J. and Henry, Z. (1944). *Doll Play of Pilaga Indian Children*. New York: American Orthopsychiatric Association.

Herrnstein, R. and Murray, C. (1994). *The Bell Curve*. New York: Free Press.

Hewlett, B. (ed.). (1992). *Father–Child Relations: Cultural and Biosocial Contexts*. Hawthorne, NY: Aldine de Gruyter.

Hull, C. L. (1943). *Principles of Behavior*. New York: Appleton-Century-Crofts.

Kelly, V. (1989). *Peer culture and interactions among Japanese children*. Unpublished Ed.D. dissertation, Harvard University Graduate School of Education.

Konner, M. J. (1972). Aspects of the developmental ethology of a foraging people. In: *Ethological Studies of Child Behavior*, ed. N. I. Blurton Jones. Cambridge, UK: Cambridge University Press.

Konner, M. J. (1975). Relations among infants and juveniles in comparative perspective. In: *Friendship and Peer Relations*, ed. M. Lewis and L. Rosenblum. New York: John Wiley.

Laboratory of Comparative Human Cognition. (1984). Culture and cognition. In: *Carmichael's Manual of Child Psychology*, vol. II, ed. P. H. Mussen. New York: John Wiley.

Lave, J. (1990). The culture of acquisition and the practice of understanding. In: *Cultural Psychology: Essays on Comparative Human Development*, ed. J. W. Stigler, R. A. Shweder and G. Herdt. New York: Cambridge University Press.

Lave, J. and Wenger, E. (1991). *Situated Learning: Legitimate Peripheral Participation*. New York: Cambridge University Press.

Lebra, T. S. (1976). *Japanese Patterns of Behavior.* Honolulu: University of Hawaii Press.

Leiderman, P. H. and Leiderman, G. F. (1977). Familial influences on infant development in an East African agricultural community. In: *Culture and Infancy,* ed. P. H. Leiderman, S. Tulkin and A. Rosenfeld. New York: Academic Press.

LeVine, R. A. and Norman, K. (in press). The infant's acquisition of culture: early attachment re-examined from an anthropological viewpoint. In: *The Psychology of Cultural Experience: Selected Papers from the Fourth Biennial Conference of the Society for Psychological Anthropology,* ed. H. Mathews and C. Moore. New York: Cambridge University Press.

LeVine, R. A., Dixon, S., LeVine, S., Richman, A., Leiderman, P. H., Keefer, C. H. and Brazelton, T. B. (1994). *Child Care and Culture: Lessons from Africa.* New York: Cambridge University Press.

Mann, C. C. (1994). Behavioral genetics in transition. *Science,* **264,** 1686–9.

Mead, M. (1928). *Coming of Age in Samoa.* New York: William Morrow.

Mean, M. (1930). *Growing Up in New Guinea.* New York: William Morrow.

Mead, M. (1932). An investigation of the thought of primitive children, with special reference to animism. *Journal of the Royal Anthropological Institute,* **62,** 173–90.

Mead, M. (1946). Research on primitive children. In: *Manual of Child Psychology,* ed. L. Carmichael. New York: John Wiley.

Miller, N. and Dollard, J. (1941). *Social Learning and Imitation.* New Haven, Conn.: Yale Univerity Press.

Munroe, R. H. and Munroe, R. L. (1971). Household density and infant care in an East African society. *Journal of Social Psychology,* **83,** 9–13.

Mussen, P. H. (ed.). (1970). *Carmichael's Manual of Child Psychology,* 3rd edn, vols I and II. New York: John Wiley.

Mussen, P. H. (ed.). (1984). *Carmichael's Manual of Child Psychology,* 4th edn, vols I–IV. New York: John Wiley.

Norman, K. (1991). *A Sound Family Makes a Sound State: Ideology and Upbringing in a German Village.* Stockholm: Department of Social Anthropology, Univerity of Stockholm.

Ochs, E. and Schieffelin, B. (1984). Language acquisition and socialization: three developmental stories. In: *Culture Theory,* ed. R. Shweder and R. LeVine. New York: Cambridge University Press.

Osofsky, J. D. (ed.). (1987). *Handbook of Infant Development.* New York: John Wiley.

Plomin, R., DeFries, J. C. and McClearn, G. E. (1990). *Behavioral Genetics.* New York: W. H. Freeman.

Rogoff, B. (1990). *Apprenticeship in Thinking: Cognitive Development in Social Context.* New York: Oxford University Press.

Rogoff, B., Mistry, J., Goncu, A. and Mosier, C. (1993). *Guided Participation in*

*Cultural Activity by Toddlers and Caregivers.* Monographs of the Society for Research in Child Development, Serial No. 236, vol. 58, No. 8. Chicago: University of Chicago Press.

Scarr, S. (1992). Developmental theories for the 1990s: development and individual differences. Biennial Meetings of the Society for Research in Child Development Presidential Address (1991, Seattle, Washington). *Child Development*, **63**, 1–19.

Schieffelin, B. and Ochs, E. (eds). (1986). *Language Socialization Across Cultures.* New York: Cambridge University Press.

Seymour, S. (1975). Child-rearing in India: a case study in change and modernization. In: *Socialization and Communication in Primary Groups*, ed. T. R. Williams. The Hague: Mouton.

Shahar, S. (1990). *Childhood in the Middle Ages.* London: Routledge.

Shwalb, D. W. and Shwalb, B. J. (eds). (1996). *Japanese Childrearing: Two Generations of Scholarship.* New York: Guilford Press.

Shweder, R. A., Shweder, J. D., Hatano, G., LeVine, R. A., Markus, H. Z. and Miller, P. (1997). The cultural psychology of child development. In: *Handbook of Child Psychology*, ed. W. Damon. New York: John Wiley.

Super, C. (1976). Environmental influences on motor development: the case of 'African infant precocity'. *Developmental Medicine and Child Neurology*, **18**, 561–7.

Super, C. and Harkness, S. (1982). The development of affect in infancy and early childhood. In: *Cultural Perspectives on Child Development*, ed. D. Wagner and H. Stevenson. San Francisco: W. H. Freeman.

Wenger, M. (1989). Work, play and social relationships among children in a Giriama community. In *Children's Social Networks and Social Supports*, ed. D. Belle. New York: John Wiley.

Weisner, T. (1989). Cultural and universal aspects of social support for children: evidence from the Abaluyia of Kenya. In: *Children's Social Networks and Social Supports*, ed. D. Bell. New York: John Wiley.

Whiting, B. B. (1963). *Six Cultures: Studies of Child Rearing.* New York: John Wiley.

Whiting, B. B. and Edwards, C. P. (1988). *Children of Different Worlds.* Cambridge, Mass.: Harvard University Press.

Whiting, B. B. and Whiting, J. W. M. (1975). *Children of Six Cultures.* Cambridge, Mass.: Harvard University Press.

Whiting, J. W. M. (1941). *Becoming a Kwoma.* New Haven, Conn.: Yale University Press.

Whiting, J. W. M. (1954). The cross-cultural method. In: *Handbook of Social Psychology*, ed. G. Lindzey. Cambridge, Mass.: Addison-Wesley.

Whiting, J. W. M. and Child, I. L. (1953). *Child Training and Personality: A Cross-Cultural Study.* New Haven, Conn.: Yale University Press.

Whiting, J. W. M., Child, I. L., Lambert, W. W., Fischer, A. M., Fischer,

J. L., Nydegger, C., Nydegger, W., Maretski, H., Maretski, T., Minturn, L., Romney, A. K. and Romney, R. (1966). *Field Guide for a Study of Socialization*. New York: John Wiley.

Wilson, E. O. (1975). *Sociobiology: The Modern Synthesis*. Cambridge, Mass.: Harvard University Press.

# 6

## *The meeting of nature and nurture and the development of children: some conclusions*

MARTIN RICHARDS

## Introduction

This volume provides readers with perspectives on childhood drawn from different traditions within the social and biological sciences. While the diversity of perspectives contributes to the richness of the offering for the reader, it also adds to the challenge posed for a discussant, at least if part of a discussant's task is to attempt to provide a linking overview as well as a commentary on the individual chapters. An analogy for the structure of this volume might be a series of journeys, each with a different starting point, but all aiming to reach the same goal: in this case an understanding of childhood and child development. Given the different terrain through which each must travel, the accounts of the journeys are necessarily different. There is a common goal and, in time, as further journeys transverse more of the surrounding country, eventually the whole country will become known and described. I suspect that this may not be a good analogy for the current status of work on childhood; perhaps we do not all share a common objective. Perhaps there is not a common objective between, for example, a view of childhood based on an aim of capturing the experience of children and another which attempts to account for the evolutionary development of childhood through natural selection. If this were correct, perhaps we are on the same journey, but we are attending to different aspects of the scenery as we travel. Perhaps we are like passengers in the same train but looking out of a window on a different side of the train. If this is a better analogy, further journeys which continue to take the different perspectives are not going to give us a picture of the whole, rather they will tend to emphasise the differences between the perspectives and the lack of common ground. On the basis that there is a reasonable case for suspicion that this may describe the situation, I suggest ways in which perspectives could shift and common ground might be created. But first some remarks on individual chapters.

## Comments on contributions

Barry Bogin attacks the idea that neoteny (or indeed other versions of heterochrony) has played a crucial part in the evolution of our own species. In this he is very much at one with the growing ideas in the exciting new field of evolutionary developmental biology (for an excellent overview, see Raff, 1996). The idea of heterochrony is a simple one: that in the development of individuals the relative timing of different developmental processes may diverge, so producing very different final body forms. Changes in timing have been thought to be a, if not the, major mechanism for the evolution of body forms. The bringing together of ideas from the study of fossils with our growing knowledge of the genes which play a part in organising developmental processes, suggest that the importance of this process has been overplayed. There has been a long tradition of writing on human evolution which has adopted heterochronic theories. In particular, the idea of neoteny has been widely accepted – that we have, in effect, retained the bodies and minds of immature apes into our adulthood. Montagu (1981), in particular, made much of this argument suggesting that not only our bodies, but much of our complex behaviour (curiosity, creativity and friendship, for instance) were features of juveniles of our primate ancestors. Following particularly the work of Shea (1989), Bogin rejects this view and instead points to evolutionary novel developments in our own evolution. He argues that childhood is one such evolutionary innovation. He adds to the older suggestion that childhood extends the period for acquiring social and technical skills and for socialisation, the sociobiological notion that it is also a feeding adaptation which may enhance parental investment and reproductive success.

Given the very little hard evidence we have about human evolution, such ideas must be speculative but in making such speculations I think it would be helpful if the question of the process by which childhood had evolved is more clearly separated from others about the social and other consequences of the emergence of this apparently novel phase of the human life cycle.

In taking his sociobiological position, Bogin has very little to say about culture, social structure or social life. He sees natural selection as the sole driving force. Once our ancestors acquired a culture, however, there are other processes to consider. This is indicated in some of the evidence against neoteny that Bogin draws on and which concern the evolution of language.

Young apes have skulls that are more similar to those of human adults than those of the adults of their own species. As Bogin describes in his chapter, the brains of apes, unlike those of humans, grow little after birth, but their faces do, producing their characteristic adult skull shape. This contrasts with the human skull where the larger cranium contains the larger brain; however, the human brain is not simply a larger version of the ape brain. Compared with chimpanzees there has been a major reorganisation associated with the development of handedness and the speech areas, among other changes (Falk, 1987). Speech implies a culture and so a complex and structured social life. Society introduces a new process into evolution which is Lamarckian rather than Darwinian.[1] The basic principles of Darwinism is a process of natural selection which operates on inherited variation, favouring differences which are adaptive in the situation in which an animal lives. Societies allow for the passing on of knowledge and skills that have been learnt

---

[1] For the sake of historical accuracy it shoud be said that Charles Darwin was a Lamarckian. He believed that characteristics acquired in a lifetime were an important source of the inherited variation on which natural selection could work. Conversely, Jean-Baptiste Lamarck made more significant contributions to evolutionary theory than the heresy that now carries his name. For the purposes of the present argument, however, I am referring to the somewhat mythical Darwin and Lamarck of modern biology.

during a lifetime. Such skills may be adaptive (or otherwise) so that there is a process of the inheritance of acquired characteristics. This Lamarckian system of cultural change is extraordinarily rapid compared with the more ponderous Darwinian process of the selection of inherited variation. Given particularly the speed of the Lamarckian process of cultural change, we are likely to considerably distort our idea of human evolution if we ignore it altogether.

Allison James describes the recent rediscovery of childhood as a social institution and ways in which this idea has become so productive for work in several disciplines. I deliberately use the term rediscovery here. The social constructionist tradition within sociology is a relatively recent development during the last couple of decades (Berger and Luckman, 1966). However, as histories of both sociology and psychology show, very similar concepts of childhood were found much earlier, as for example in the childhood study movement, especially in the United States, in the inter-war period (see Richards, 1978; Bradley, 1989). Some of this work is described in Robert LeVine's chapter. Among the many theoretical advantages of social constructionist perspective is that it challenges the somewhat unthinking universality of so much research which speaks of 'the child'. The tradition of work described here is much more sensitive to the limits of generalisation and examines the worlds of children in specific places and at specific times. In these arguments there is much common ground with Robert LeVine who suggests that psychologists, in particular, have often overgeneralised and made universal principles from studies of specific children in specific environments. In his notion of environmental optimisation, he suggests that child rearing and developmental processes will differ as parents in each society will have an agenda about how to bring up children best equipped to live in the adult world around.

What I found missing in Allison James' account was a discussion of the issues which might have led to some connection with the concept of childhood employed by Barry Bogin in his chapter. There is no necessary conflict between a notion of childhood specific to culture and time and the idea that it is an evolutionary innovation which separates us from our primate ancestors; however, some theoretical work is necessary to build a connection.

James says that 'the biological base of childhood' is now more readily acknowledged by social scientists but it is seen as a context of a
child's life rather than 'a forceful determinant of their actions'
(p. 62). I would like some more discussion of what this 'biological
base' might be and how it forms a context for a child's life. What,
for example, marks out those parts of a child that are biological
from those which are social? Can one sustain a separation between
these two concepts? These are issues I return to later.

Robert LeVine argues for a new environmentalism in child
development research. He suggests that while the concept of interaction of nature and nurture remains widely accepted, the balance
has been pushed strongly towards nurture. Indeed, he suggests that
there is a danger that the environmentalist cause has been irretriev-
ably lost. To prevent this, he describes work in which he and colleagues have been involved to build what they refer to as a new
environmentalism based on the evidence of divergent pathways of
behavioural development of the child in different cultural settings
and the notion of environmental optimisation. Evidence of just such
pathways is provided in the chapter by Catherine Panter-Brick in
her discussion of child health and the means by which it may be
monitored and measured. At first sight it might seem a rather
simple matter to create indicators that might be used across cultures
to monitor health, or its absence. In the more extreme case it is
easy, but as soon as we begin to ask rather more specific questions
about well-being or growth, for instance, matters become both a
great deal more complicated and culturally dependent, as the chapter shows. In this chapter, as in the one by Robert LeVine, the
environment, both social and physical, is seen as a context in which
children grow up and develop. Both take a position of interaction
of nature and nurture as an underlying assumption, though Rober
LeVine, in particular, wants to argue for a change in where the
balance between these two interacting factors is.

This same interactionist position is at the root of Allison James'
remarks about the biological bases of childhood and Barry Bogin's
discussion of the evolution of childhood. In the final part of these
remarks I argue that wc must move beyond the concept of an
interaction of nature and nurture to a conceptualisation which is

more in tune with our understanding of biological and, indeed social, development. I believe that these matters have become more urgent not least because of the argument that Rober LeVine makes that a 'new innatism' is now promoted. I believe that Robert LeVine is correct when he states that part of the reason for this new innatism is the rapid developments in molecular genetics that have occurred over the past two or three decades. While there is nothing in these developments which in themselves imply a change in attitudes, if anything quite the reverse, the change arises from the ways in which these new developments in molecular genetics are talked about. I first elaborate that point and then return to the much wider question of nature, nurture and interactionism in relation to the development of children.

## Talking about genes

In most discussions, the origin and the driving force for the processes of development are located firmly within the biological world. The common conceptualisation in psychology and elsewhere in the social sciences is that we begin our lives as biological beings who are then made social, or at least are given a social veneer, by the process of development. This process is often referred to as socialisation, the taming of a biological being. As I have mentioned, this perspective which gives priority to biology has been strongly reinforced by a number of recent developments, especially in molecular biology. The growing understanding of gene action at a molecular level does not give direct reinforcement to biological primacy, rather this comes through the ways in which this area of science is often discussed. DNA has not just become an icon of science (Nelkin and Lindee, 1995), but is increasingly seen as the beginning and end of all processes in the living world. Within popular culture and many scientific discussions DNA has been endowed with both mystical properties and even human emotions. DNA is not only the secret of life, its blueprint, but it has powers of self-replication and a selfish character, or so we are frequently told.

In popular fiction the powers of this molecule become even more remarkable. According to the story of the popular film, *Jurassic Park*, fragments of fossil DNA can, with the help of some fast footwork from molecular biologists, be turned into living animals. It is, of course, a fiction, and not even a technology that might play a part in any reasonably imagined future, but it does chime with the ways in which many biologists and their popularisers discuss DNA. There is talk of genes 'for' many things: intelligence, schizophrenia, breast cancer, criminality, eye colour or even divorce. The implication of such talk is that residing in our DNA are the instructions and the powers to create these characteristics. Implicit in many current notions of genes for characteristics is a deterministic one-to-one relation between the gene and the character: between genotype and phenotype; but genes are merely DNA base pairs which are involved in the process of arranging amino acid sequences in proteins. In developmental terms that is a very long way from the (phenotypic) characteristics for which the gene is said to stand. It is not simply a matter of developmental distance between the genes and the phenotypic characters that are important here, the need is also to recognise that the developmental processes are not of a kind that can be described by a linear causality. Genes do not produce red hair or any other character in a direct way because there are all sorts of influences above the cellular level that form part of the process. For example, development may depend on the position of a cell in relation to other cells and its orientation in relation to the body as a whole (Wolpert, 1991). Furthermore, genes cannot be considered as independent operators. They themselves are part of the organism and their activity, or lack of it, is determined by the nature of other genes, biochemical processes within the cell and all sorts of influences beyond the cell wall and, indeed, the body of the organism.

Much more is inherited than DNA. In the human case, we pass between generations a lot of other cell contents beyond the genes. Most importantly we inherit a structured social environment and a culture in which we may grow up. This is the rapid Lamarckian inheritance I mentioned earlier. As Oyama (1991) has put it, 'there can be no distinction between behaviour that is "in the gene" and behaviour that is "acquired" . . .'. In short, genes are part of a developmental system in which each part is dependent on the rest of the system. We can, of course, correlate variations in characteristics with either genetic or environmental variation but the developmental processes cannot be categorised in terms of this dualism.

Evolutionary change may be charted by changing gene frequencies in populations of individuals over time. Some have taken this useful and uncontroversial idea and turned it into the radical fundamentalist notion that the genes are the motor of evolution (Gould, 1992). Dawkins (1976) expresses this idea by referring to genes as the 'replicators' and organisms as the 'vehicles' that carry them. So animals become the genes' way of making more genes and genes are enthroned as the central players of the biological and evolutionary world. While biologists and philosophers (e.g. Sober and Lewontin, 1982; Sterelny and Kitchen, 1988) have widely criticised this ultra-Darwinist reductionism, the notion hangs on in both scientific and lay discussions and reinforces the idea that the genes are the beginning and end of life. While more satisfactory theoretical positions may not be as conceptually simple, many biologists do not accept that there is an exclusive unit of selection as Dawkins claims for the genes. As Gould (1992: 47) states, 'nature is organised as a hierarchy – genes in organisms, organisms in populations, and populations in species. Entities at each level of the hierarchy can act as biological "individuals" and Darwin's process of selection can therefore occur at all levels, with none dominant in all situations'.

## Beyond the interaction of nature and nurture

As we have seen, many discussions of childhood and the development of children are couched in the conceptualisation of nature (or the genes) and nurture (or the environment). For most characteristics, nobody claims total genetic or environmental determinism, rather most espouse some version of 'interactionism' which involve these two conceptual categories of nature and nurture acting with each other in a developmental process. There will be differences, however, in the extent to which one or other set of factors are emphasised ('it's largely genetic', 'there is little evidence for inherited factors', etc.). The basic theoretical point which I argue here is that the conceptualisation into the two categories (the genetic and the environmental, or nature and nurture) provides a misleading and unhelpful model of children's (biological and social) development. Despite attempts stretching back to the last century to replace the dichotomy of nature and nurture with other models, it is still widely used. As one recent theorist of developmental psychology has put it, 'Indeed "nature vs nurture" is less a dichotomy than a sprawling complex of multiple interconnected beliefs, metaphors and associations. It is not easily disposed of, for it is deeply embedded in our thought, and it has as many conceptual relatives as it has guises' (Oyama, 1991: 28). Although there have been numerous discussions of the inadequacies of the two concepts in this dualism and the meaninglessness of the idea of interaction, the interactionist approach lives on as a dominant position in work on the development of children. Old habits die hard and discussions seem often to begin and end with the dichotomy. There are, of course, alternatives; perhaps less finely detailed theoretical statements than an overlapping series of positions with common features, which may trade under the names of constructionism, epigenesis or developmental systems approaches and are associated with authors such as Lewontin et al. (1984), Oyama (1985), Gottlieb (1991) and Gray (1992) among many others. I turn to these in the final part of this discussion. First, however, it is necessary to say a little more about the contribution of studies which do employ the conceptualisation of nature and nurture.

The classic quantitative technique for investigating these issues is the calculations of heritabilities. The heritability of a trait is the proportion of variance in that trait that may be accounted for (in statistical terms) by genetic variation within the particular population. It is thus based on a statistical model that partitions all variance into either nature or nurture. As Robert LeVine noted in his chapter, measures of heritability are specific to the population (in genetic terms) and environment from which the measured individuals came. It is also important to underline that it is a statistic describing variance in a population, so only very indirectly, if at all, will it link to any developmental process. Heritability

Table 6.1. *Genetic component, shared environmental and unshared environmental components in the variance in scenes for a number of different measures of psychosocial coping in children to self-reported events in the family and the school*

| Coping strategies | Genetic component | Shared environmental component | Unshared environmental component |
|---|---|---|---|
| Distraction | 0.99 | 0.00 | 0.01 |
| Use of parents | 0.53 | 0.01 | 0.46 |
| Use of peers | 0.18 | 0.00 | 0.82 |
| Problem solve | 0.00 | 0.15 | 0.85 |
| Self-soothe | 0.53 | 0.00 | 0.47 |
| Problem-focused | 0.57 | 0.06 | 0.37 |
| Emotion-focused | 0.00 | 0.99 | 0.01 |

*Source:* from Mellins et al. (1996).

calculations can have some value in pointing to where we might usefully begin in trying to unravel a developmental process. This might be illustrated by a recent study of children's methods of coping with stress (Mellins et al., 1996). This study involved 44 monozygotic and 30 dizygotic twin pairs, aged 9–16 years, drawn from the South California Twins Project. The ways in which children cope with psychosocial stress was assessed in an interview which focused on recent stressful events in the family and at school, such as having difficulties with a teacher or being rejected by peers. Coping skills were also assessed by questionnaire in relation to the specific stressful events reported by the children. Heritabilities were calculated for seven coping variables using a model that distinguishes in statistical terms between shared (those common to both twins) and unshared (those unique to one child of the twin pair) environmental factors. What the results showed was that heritabilities for the different coping variables will be very different and that, for all but one of them, the unshared environment was more significant than the shared environment (Table 6.1). While we have to be a little cautious in using such statistical models as a way of understanding developmental processes,[2] this would suggest that as well as investigating shared family environments, we are to build models which might explain individual differences in coping ability, and we should pay a lot of attention to experiences unique to individual children in the family. Useful though this signpost might be, however, it does not get us far if our goal were to explain why some children are much better at coping with some stresses than others.

The development of techniques which (statistically) separate the shared and unshared components in the variance that may be attributed to environmental factors in heritability studies have been widely deployed in recent years (Plomin, 1994). Many of these studies show that for characteristics such as personality and cognitive abilities almost all the variance in measures that may be attributed to environmental factors may be assigned to the non-shared environment (Plomin et al., 1994). The implication of these findings is not that family and parental factors are unimportant to children but that different family experiences are influenced by the same processes or events in different ways. From the point of view of the argument I present here, these findings are important, for they support the position that theoretical arguments based on any simple notion of interaction of nature and nurture are not likely to get us very far.

As far as genes are concerned, almost all the single genes known to influence psychological or psychiatric characteristics are, in essence, major disruptors of developmental systems. This, of course, makes them extraordinarily important in clinical terms, but means they are rather unilluminating of developmental processes. Effectively, conditions like phenylketonuria or Huntington's disease can be regarded as spanners in the works. The identification of the gene mutations involved in such conditions and an understanding of the biochemical pathways involved has been very valuable for our understanding of the spanners, but little help in learning more of

---

[2] A further reason for caution here is that measurement error will appear as part of the unshared environment component. Most recently a 'maternal effects' model for heritability has been proposed which gives a better fit to data and suggests we may have grossly overestimated the heritability of IQ and probably many other characters (Devlin et al., 1997).

works they disrupt. In the case of phenylketonuria the 'spanner' is an inability to metabolise the amino acid phenylalanine. This is one of the building blocks of proteins which is found in many foods. If children with this disease eat foods which contain phenylalanine, chemicals accumulate in their body which damage their developing brain. Knowledge of this particular spanner has provided a way of preventing the brain damage which characterises this inherited disease. Children are put on a diet which minimises their intake of phenylalanine and their brains develop in a normal way. This is one of the sadly rare success stories in genetic disease where an effective cure is available. From the point of view of the argument I put forward here, while providing the special diet for children with the condition allows their normal development, it has not led to any great increased understanding of the ways in which children's brains develop.

There are many psychological attributes and psychiatric conditions which estimates suggest have significant heritabilities, such as IQ or schizophrenia; however, all we can say about their inheritance is it does not follow simple Mendelian patterns (Hall, 1996). Indeed, perhaps that is exactly the point. The development processes in childhood that link gene action to a behavioural trait are long and little understood. A full description of the process would involve a whole series of levels of analysis, including the genome, the cell, the individual, social relationship and culture. It would be very odd if such a process could be reduced to a simple cause and effect chain unless we were talking about factors, at whatever level, that represented massive disruptors of the whole process.

## Constructionism and the system's view of child development

Epigenetic systems approaches to development do not begin with an idea of two realms, the biological and the social, which are then brought into some kind of relation with each other. They thus avoid all the problems of trying to define and separate these two worlds. Instead they begin with a notion of a system in which there are multiple interconnections and which is hierarchically organised into multiple levels from societies through individuals to cells and their chemical constituents. Mutual influence is to be found at all levels. Developmental processes continue across time. For their analysis, we need a starting and end point. However, we may be misled if these points are defined as conception and death. From an epigenetic point of view we might equally begin with the formation of two gametes which ultimately come together at fertilisation or the glance across the room that led to the first social encounter of the woman and man who later conceived a child. The causal origin of developmental processes cannot be located at any particular place within the development system. Development would not proceed without the contributions of DNA from both egg and sperm but neither would it if the integrity of the cell arising from the fertilisation were broached, or indeed if the mother and father had decided against penetrative sex on the occasion at which fertilisation occurred.

As I have mentioned it is often suggested that genes have a special part to play in all developmental processes as they provide the information, the blueprint, for development. From this perspective, genes indeed do occupy the centre stage in which they have a unique organisational role which is played out against a (biological and social) environment. There is no information which might control development which is contributed by the genes. Rather the control of development is diffused throughout the entire developmental system. As Gray (1992) states, 'development is a contingent, conditional process. This claim builds on the basic truism of joint determination. It notes that the effects of both genetic and environmental differences are contingent on the context in which they occur ... The impact of an environmental factor will vary depending on the developmental state of the organism and, reciprocally, the effect of a gene being activated will depend on the state of the rest of the developmental system ... The reciprocal and temporal contingency of developmental causation not the simple addition of a genetic and an environmental vector ... Developmental causation must therefore be conceptualised in system rather than vector terms' (pp. 175–6).

The term 'constructionist' arises from the idea that phenotypes are constructed anew each generation as children grow up. Traits are not transmitted from generation to generation. Rather a series of potential interactive processes pass from generation to generation. Genes do not pass on information or instruction for development of a new child, instead the information arises as a part of developmental systems. Susan Oyama underlines the point in the title of her book *The Ontogeny of Information* (Oyama, 1985). In her phrase, 'information itself has an ontogeny'.

Conceptualising development in systems terms suggests a degree of uncertainty in the characteristics of phenotype. Certainly children are never identical with either parent, or indeed some theoretical mid-point or mixture of their characters; however, there are clear broad consistencies and resemblances. The consistencies reside in the process of development, they are not specified outcomes. Processes that favour consistency have been conceptualised in a number of ways. Several developmental psychologists have found Waddington's (1957) concept of canalisation useful in this context. Waddington argued that many developmental processes are buffered in such a way that as they depart from a pathway there are increasing pressures to return. Waddington often used the analogy of a ballbearing rolling down a valley to illustrate this process. The ballbearing hits an obstruciton in the floor of the valley and bounces up one side. The slope brings it back to the floor of the valley (Gottlieb, 1991).

## Conclusion

The theoretical issues concerning the processes of the development of children may sometimes seem a long way from the discussion of childhood. My contention is that, if we are to find a common ground on which we could stand to discuss the issues about childhood raised by the contributors to this volume, we must reject concepts of nature and nurture and replace these with a constructionist or epigenetic perspective. This volume with its perspective drawn from a number of different traditions provides a strong push in that direction. The focus here is on the diversity of cultures and of individual experiences of children. This work raises exciting new challenges which demand a new perspective. That is the promise that lies beyond the traditional conceptualisation of nature and nurture.

# References

Berger, P. and Luckman, T. (1966). *The Social Construction of Reality*. New York: Doubleday.

Bradley, B. S. (1989) *Visions of Infancy: A Critical Introduction to Child Psychology*. Cambridge: Cambridge University Press.

Devlin, B., Daniels, M. and Roeders, K. (1997). The heritability of IQ. *Nature*, **388**, 468–471.

Falk, D. (1987). Brain lateralization in primates and its evolution in humans. *Yearbook of Physical Anthropology*, **30**, 107–25.

Gottlieb, G. (1991). Experiential canalization of behavioral development in theory. *Developmental Psychology*, **27**, 4–13.

Gould, S. J. (1992). The confusion over evolution. *The New York Review of Books*, **19**, 47–54.

Gray, R. (1992). Death of the gene: developmental systems strike back. In: *Trees of Life*, ed. P. Griffiths. The Hague: Kluwer.

Hall, L. L. (ed.). (1996). *Genetics and Mental Illness*. New York: Plenum Press.

Lewontin, R. C., Rose, S. and Kamin, L. F. (1984). *Not in Our Genes: Biology, Ideology, and Human Nature*. London: Penguin.

Mellins, C. A., Gatz, M. and Baker, L. (1996). Children's methods of coping with stress: a twin study of genetic and environmental influences. *Journal of Child Psychology and Psychiatry*, **37**, 721–30.

Montagu, M. F. A. (1981). *Growing Young*. New York: McGraw-Hill.

Nelkin, D. and Lindee, M. S. (1995). *The DNA Mystique. The Gene as a Cultural Icon*. New York: Freeman.

Oyama, S. (1985). *The Ontogeny of Information*. Cambridge: Cambridge University Press.

Oyama, S. (1991). Bodies and minds: dualism in evolutionary theory. *Journal of Social Issues*, **47**, 27–42.

Plomin, R. (1994). *Genetics and Experience. The Interplay between Nature and Nurture*. Newbury Park, CA: Sage.

Plomin, R., Chipver, H. M. and Niederheiser, J. M. (1994). Behavioral genetic evidence for the importance of non-shared environment. In: *Separate Social Worlds of Siblings*, ed. E. M. Hetherington, D. Reiss and R Plomin. Hillsdale, NJ: Erlbaum.

Raff, R. A. (1996). *The Shape of Life. Genes, Development and the Evolution of Animal Form.* Chicago: University of Chicago Press.

Richards, M. P. M. (1978). The biological and the social. In: *Action, Gesture and Symbol*, ed. A. Lock. Academic Press.

Richards, M. P. M. (ed.). (1994). *The Integration of a Child into a Social World.* Cambridge: Cambridge University Press.

Shea, B. T. (1989). Heterochrony in human evolution: the case for neotomy reconsidered. *Yearbook of Physical Anthropology*, **32**, 69–101.

Sober, E. and Lewontin, R. C. (1982). Artifact, cause and genic selection. *Philosophy of Science*, **49**,157–80.

Sterelny, K. and Kitchen, P. (1988). The return of the gene. *Journal of Philosophy*, **85**, 338–61.

Waddington, C. H. (1957). *The Strategy of the Genes.* London: Allen and Unwin.

Wahisten, D. (1990). Insensitivity of the analysis of variance to heredity: environment interaction. *Behavioural and Brain Sciences*, **13**,109–61.

Wolpert, L. (1991). *The Triumph of the Embryo.* Oxford: Oxford University Press.

# Glossary

**accommodation** an individual's response to environmental challenge that is not wholly successful: although promoting survival, it results in significant costs in short-term or long-term function

**adaptability** the ability of an individual to mount beneficial responses to environmental challenges, which are reversible and reflect biological flexibility or plasticity

**adaptation** a beneficial change on the part of an individual to mitigate specific environmental challenges; the responses may have a biological or cultural basis. As distinct from accommodation, the benefits of an adaptive response must outweigh associated costs in the short and long term

**adolescence** human developmental stage following puberty; marked by the development of secondary sexual characteristics, the onset of serious attempts at adult sociosexual and economic behaviour and, usually, a growth spurt in both height and weight

**adulthood** stage of the life cycle when either growth in size is complete and/or full reproductive maturation is complete; the state of full social maturity

**adrenaline** a hormone secreted by the adrenal medulla in response to perceived physical or psychosocial stress, which raises heart rate, blood pressure and circulating levels of glucose and lipids in preparation for 'flight' or 'fight'; also called epinephrine

**adrenarche** the onset of secretion of adrenal androgen hormones, known to occur only in chimpanzees, during their juvenile growth stage, and in humans during their childhood growth stage

**allometry** the study of the growth of part of an organism in relation to the growth of the entire organism; also, a change in proportion of any of the parts of an organism that occurs during growth

**anthropometry** measurement of the human body

**attachment theory** a school of thought, developed by John Bowlby in the 1950s, based on the idea of an enduring social attachment of mother and infant established in the first year of life; lack of such attachment is claimed to lead to a failure to form normal adult social relationships

**australopithecine** an extinct grade in hominid evolution found principally in eastern and southern Africa, including *Australopithecus afarensis* (an early form, dating to about 5.5 million years ago) and *Australopithecus africanus* (a species dating from approximately 3.5 million years ago to about 1.6 million years ago

**behaviourism** a school of psychology that concerns itself with the objective observation of an individual's behaviour and the direct links between response and stimulus

**childhood** stage of human development between infancy and adolescence (or between birth and adulthood)

**cortisol** the principal glucocorticoid hormone secreted by the adrenal cortex in response to positive or negative feelings of arousal; affects energy release, immune function and mental activity

**Darwinian theory** the theory of the origin of plant and animal species through a process of evolution by natural selection

**Declaration of the Rights of the Child** seeks to secure children's rights, which can be summarised into three types: the right to survival, the right to protection and the right to development (outlined at the end of this glossary). The Declaration (1959) was adopted by the United Nations General Assembly in 1989. This transformed 'soft law' (a declaration) into 'hard law' (a Convention) demanding ratification on the part of individual countries.

**demography** the scientific study of human populations, especially with reference to their size, structure and spatial distribution

**developmental plasticity** the ability of an individual to modify a trait (often one that is under genetic control) during the growth period

**ecological variables** factors in the natural and cultural environment that affect the characteristics of individuals and populations; ecological variables thus pertain to the relationships between individuals and all aspects of their environment

**encephalisation quotient** a mathematical expression of the amount of central nervous system tissue, especially the brain, that an animal possesses above that amount expected for the body size of a 'typical' mammal

**endocrine system** all the body's hormone secreting glands, such as the pituitary, thyroid, testes, ovaries, pineal and adrenal glands

**environmentalism** the belief that a person's characteristics and behaviour are affected chiefly by the environment

**epidemiology** the branch of medical science concerned with the occurrence, transmission and control of infectious diseases

**epigenesis** the theory that an individual animal or plant develops by the gradual differentiation and elaboration of a fertilised egg cell

**epinephrine** see adrenaline

**evolution** change, for example a change in gene frequency in a population from one generation to the next

**extant** still in existence; surviving, as opposed to extinct

**gene** the unit of biological heredity; a segment of DNA that codes for the synthesis of a single protein

**genetic determinism** the belief that a person's characteristics and behaviour are largely the product of genes

**genotype** the inherited genetic make-up of a particular individual; in contrast to expressed characteristics or phenotype

**growth** a quantitative increase in cell number, cell size or mass

    **catch-up** a period of rapid growth following a period of slow or absent growth (growth faltering) usually due to the correction of a physical or emotional condition that retards growth

    **distance** the amount of growth achieved in a given time period

    **spurt** a relatively sudden and noticeable increase in the rate of growth, usually reaching a peak and declining back to the pre-spurt rate of growth

    **velocity** the rate at which an individual grows during a given time period

**height-for-age** measure of an individual's growth status (height in metres relative to age), which largely reflects the adequacy of past environmental conditions; see stunting

**heritability** the relative amount of variation in a trait due to genetic causes as a fraction of total variance in observed characteristics (phenotype), the total variance being due to genes, the environment and their interactions

**heterochrony** changes in the timing of developmental events or stages that produce changes in observed characteristics or phenotype

**hominid** popular form of *Hominidae*, from homo (man); the family to which ancestral and living humans belong, characterised by bipedality

***Homo erectus*** hominid form that is the direct ancestor of *Homo sapiens*; appearing about 1.9 million years ago and flourishing until about 200 000 to 250 000 years ago. *H. erectus* was at least five feet tall, with a body and limbs that were within the range of variation of modern humans, and had a cranial capacity ranging from 900 to 1200 cubic centimetres

***Homo habilis* ('handy man')** a fossil form, dating from more than two million years ago; the earliest hominid with which stone tools have been found in unambiguous relationship

***Homo sapiens*** two subspecies: *neanderthalensis*, commonly known as Neanderthal man, appearing some 300 000 years ago and becoming extinct about 35 000 years ago; *sapiens*, all contemporary humans, first appearing about 60 000 years ago

**hominoid** popular form of *Hominoidea*; the superfamily to which all ancestral and living human and ape species belong

**hormones** proteins produced by specialised cells that travel to other parts of body where they influence chemical reactions

**hypermorphosis** delay in the termination of developmental stages, thereby prolonging the duration and effect of each stage on an individual's growth and development

**infancy** earliest period of life after birth; stage of development when the young are dependent on maternal lactation (in mammals); from the Latin *infans*: without speech

**innatism** see genetic determinism

**juvenile** an immature individual; among the social mammals, a pre-pubertal individual no longer dependent on other individuals for survival

**Lamarckian theory** the notion developed by Lamarck that traits acquired during the lifetime of an organism could be passed on to offspring

**learning theory** a formulation (by Clark Hull in 1957) of stimulus–response theory, applied to human behaviour

**maximal oxygen consumption** (or maximal aerobic capacity, $\dot{V}O_2max$). The ability to extract and utilise oxygen is measured for individuals close to exhaustion during a graded work test on a bicycle ergometer, treadmill or standard steptest. The relationships between heart rates, oxygen consumption and physical work capacity have been studied extensively

**menarche** the first menstrual bleeding, or period

**morbidity** the affliction of illnesses that fall short of death or mortality

**natural selection** the evolutionary factor, first articulated by Charles Darwin, that causes changes in gene frequencies in populations due to the differential reproductive success of individuals

**nature–nurture debate** the controversy regarding the extent to which genetic (nature) and environmental (nurture) factors shape a person's characteristics and behaviour

**neoteny** retention of larval or foetal features in the adult form of an animal

**ontogeny** the entire sequence of events involved in the development of an individual

**phenotype** the observable or measurable characteristic of an individual

**puberty** the achievement of sexual maturity; an event of the neuroendocrine system that marks the onset of sexual maturation; from the Latin *pubescere*: to grow hair

**'selfish gene' hypothesis** the proposition that most animal behaviour is selected to increase the fitness of the self at the expense of others

**social constructionist approach** the idea that culture is reinvented by each generation as individuals actively construct a social world through social interactions

**'strange situation'** a technique developed by Mary Ainsworth to measure attachment (see attachment theory) which involves placing a child in a strange environment with or without the company of the mother or an adult stranger

**stress** challenge from the physical or social environment that affects an individual

**stunting** short height in response to poor environmental conditions such as undernutrition and infection; measured as low height-for-age

**synergy** the working together of two or more conditions to produce a more powerful effect (an effect greater than the sum of their individual effects)

**twin studies** the use of identical (monozygotic) and non-identical (dizygotic) twins to study the relative contribution of genetic and environmental effects on the development of a given characteristic

**wasting** low weight resulting from breakdown of fat and/or muscle, due to starvation; measured as low weight-for-height

**weaning** the first introduction of supplementary food; alternatively, the termination of breast-feeding

**weight-for-age** measure of an individual's growth status (weight in kilograms relative to age); does not differentiate stunting (short height) from wasting (low weight-for-height)

**weight-for-height** measure of an individual's growth status (weight in kilograms divided by height in metres) which is independent of age

**World Summit of Children (1990)** specified social goals for 1995 and the year 2000. The goals for the end of this century (summarised under ten priority points at the end of this glossary) were agreed by almost all the world's governments

# The Declaration of the Rights of the Child (1959)
## (from The Rights of the Child, UNICEF video, 1989)

1  The right to equality, regardless of race, religion, nationality or sex.
2  The right to special protection for full physical, intellectual, moral, spiritual and social development in a healthy and normal manner.
3  The right to a name and nationality.
4  The right to adequate nutrition, housing and medical services.
5  The right to special care, if handicapped.
6  The right to love, understanding and protection.
7  The right to free education, to play and recreation.
8  The right to be among the first to receive relief in times of disaster.
9  The right to protection against all forms of neglect, cruelty and exploitation.
10 The right to protection from any form of discrimination, and the right to be brought up in a spirit of universal brotherhood, peace and tolerance.

## The World Summit for Children (1990)
summarised under ten priority points (from UNICEF –
The State of the World's Children, 1996: 72)

1 A one-third reduction in 1990 under-five death rates (or to 70 per 1000 live births, whichever is less).
2 A halving of 1990 maternal mortality rates.
3 A halving of 1990 rates of malnutrition among the world's under-fives (to include the elimination of micro-nutrient deficiencies, support for breast-feeding by all maternity units and a reduction in the incidence of low birth weights to less than 10%).
4 The achievement of 90% immunisation among under-ones, the eradication of polio, the elimination of neonatal tetanus, a 90% reduction in measles cases and a 95% reduction in measles deaths (compared with pre-immunisation levels).
5 A halving of child deaths caused by diarrhoeal diseases.
6 A one-third reduction in child deaths from acute respiratory infections.
7 Basic education for all children and completion of primary education by at least 80%: girls as well as boys.
8 Safe water and sanitation for all communities.
9 Acceptance by all countries of the Convention on the Rights of the child, including improved protection for children in especially difficult circumstances.
10 Universal access to high-quality family planning information and services in order to prevent pregnancies that are too early, too closely spaced, too late or too many.

# Index of selected authors

# Index of ethnographic examples

Agta 33
Aka 33

Bangladesh 69, 81, 85
Botswana 107

Caribbean 89–90, 114
Chewong 57
Colombia 84

Denmark 60
Dominica 89

East Africa 112

Gambia (The) 68, 73–4, 86
Germany 6, 120–2, 124
Guatemala 33, 107
Gusii 6, 117–22, 124

Hadza 32–3, 86

India 85, 107
Inuit 5, 50, 57
Ireland 84

Japan 5–6, 50–1, 122, 125
Java 85

Kenya 6, 70, 85, 117

Kipsigi 85–6
!Kung 20, 31, 33, 86

Liberia 107

Malay 57
Manus 106
Maya 33
Mexico 107
Micronesia 114

Nepal 68, 69, 73, 81, 83–6, 92

Papua New Guinea 74, 106
Peru 58, 74, 81
Philippines 33, 107

Quechua 86

Samoa 106
Senegal 69, 83–4
Sierra Leone 114
Six Cultures Study 106–7, 112
Sweden 125

Tanzania 31
Trinidad and Tabago 48
Turkana 70–1, 80

UK 50–1, 55, 60, 82, 92

# Subject index

accommodation 75
adaptability 79, 93
adaptation 29–30, 34, 37, 75, 133
adolescence 18, 19, 23, 24, 27, 103,
    116
  *see also* growth spurt
adrenaline 92
adrenarche 19
adult
  views on child 1–2, 4–5
  adulthood 17–19, 23, 25, 51, 59
  *see also* brain size, caregiving,
    evolutionary success, neoteny
allometry 35
alloparental care 67, 88
anthropometry 67, 70–5
attachment theory 48, 105, 122

birth intervals 31–2, 34, 69–70
brain size or development 20–2,
    25–30, 35, 133, 142
breast-feeding 3, 19–20, 81, 112,
    117

caregiving practices 6, 37–40, 70,
    78, 94, 114, 118–21
  *see also* infancy, parental goals and
    investment
'cerebral Rubicon' 27–9
child-centred perspectives 1–2, 51,
    57–8, 62

childhood,
  age range 3–4, 21, 62, 66–7,
    03
  biological or evolutionary basis 4,
    Chapter 2 *passim*, 132–5
  definitions *see* age-range, social
    constructs
  social constructs or cultural
    models 2–3, 5–7, Chapter 3
    *passim*, 118–24, 134–5
  *see also* adolescence, adulthood,
    infancy, juvenile stage,
    child-centred perspectives
children
  as participants in adult life 5, 51,
    56–8, 61, 120–1
  as social actors 47, 52–8, 59
  as the next generation 49–50, 58
  'at risk' 30, 50–1, 57, 66, 69, 75
  their dependency or self-reliance
    6, 32, 50, 58, 121
  their health Chapter 4 *passim*
  their resilience or vulnerability 6,
    21, 48, 66, 69–70, 79, 93
  their needs 4, 22, 34, 49, 52, 58,
    94
  their rights 52, 54–5, 94, 151–2
  their work and physical activity
    58, 81–9, 94, 121
  *see also* education, development,
    growth, play